CP 1st 7⁵⁰

AND IT WAS MORNING

by Poul Borchsenius

THE SON OF A STAR

AND IT WAS MORNING

THE STORY OF THE
JEWS IN OUR TIME

POUL BORCHSENIUS

TRANSLATED BY REGINALD SPINK

ILLUSTRATED

Ruskin House
GEORGE ALLEN & UNWIN LTD
MUSEUM STREET LONDON

PRINTED IN GREAT BRITAIN
IN 12 ON 13 PT. CENTAUR TYPE
BY JARROLD AND SONS LTD
NORWICH

CONTENTS

꒳

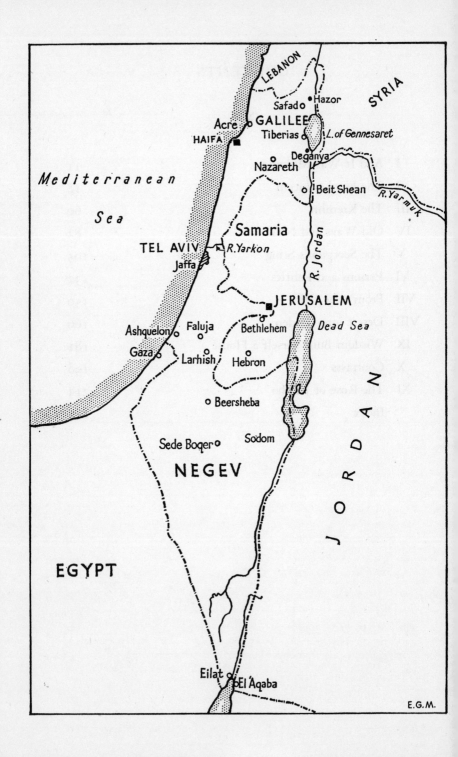

ILLUSTRATIONS

I

AND IT WAS MORNING

❧

A NEW day dawned over Tel Aviv. The stars had already paled, and one by one the myriad twinkling lights went out—the same stars which Abraham had seen on the night he had received the promise that his seed would be as numerous and would inherit the land they watched over. The sky turned transparent and azure-blue as, away in the east, the sun's disc rose above the dark hills of Judaea, sending its rays across the plain towards the sea like the ripples of a smile. Suddenly, palms and cypresses, disengaging themselves from the dark night, stood erect in the daylight, while orange groves, cactus hedges, and green fields emerged from the mist. And then at last the sun reached the coast, where it shone on a confusion of houses down by the shore. It was morning in Tel Aviv, a morning in May.

It is in May that Tel Aviv should be seen. The city can be very impressive in the hot and humid summer; but in May when the sun is still young, it is carpeted with flowers so that it glows like a painter's palette. Trees and flowers—pines, palms, hibiscuses, magnolias, oleanders, bougainvilleas, mimosas —growing in innumerable little gardens along the rows of houses, brighten the uniform streets. In winter they provide shelter, and when spring comes round the city puts on a floral coat of brilliant colours.

The flowers apart, Tel Aviv might be thought a plain city. Completely new, it lacks the patina which in an old town can invest even ugliness with the charm of age. But the visitor with an eye for modern art soon realizes that it is a fine example of

contemporary architecture. It is functionalistic, the houses
standing in cool, severe lines like match-boxes piled one on top
of the other or stood upright. The place had to be built quickly
and cheaply; and so here are these concrete blocks with their
large, regular wall surfaces in every shade of sand—white,
yellow, and grey—and with the flats hidden behind deep balconies. In Israel this method has proved practical, suiting the
climate. There the task of the architects is not, as it is in the
North, to conserve warmth, but to exclude the humid heat.
They have discharged it well; for in Tel Aviv it is cool
inside.

Incredibly but true, on the site now occupied by miles of
boulevards, and blocks of houses accommodating nearly half a
million inhabitants, there were, half a century ago, only
desolate sand dunes. This purely Jewish city, the only one in
the world, recently celebrated its fiftieth anniversary.

This May morning was the start of a red-letter day in Tel
Aviv's history. One day when the story of our chaotic times
comes to be written, it will mark one of the few constructive
acts of the post-war period: the proclamation of the State of
Israel on May 14, 1948. After ancient disasters—in the year
70 when the legions of Titus stormed Jerusalem and destroyed the Temple, and again in 135 when the last sparks of the
insurrection of Simon Bar-Cochbar were stamped out under the
iron heel of Rome and the people of Israel were driven into
centuries of exile—a new Jewish State had arisen.

Tel Aviv wakes with the sun and its inhabitants are early
about. One has to take advantage of the cool morning hours
when a fresh breeze blows from the sea, fanning the city.
The crowds in the street are a motley throng, gathered together
from all over the world. Seated on the stone steps of the
synagogue there is a bearded old man with long earlocks,
hoarsely intoning Hebrew prayers, with a bowl in front of him
for alms. A Yemenite couple will pass by, slim, dark, and
handsome, the woman wearing a gold-embroidered gown, and
Oriental ornaments round her neck, wrists, and ankles. They
are followed by dark-complexioned Jews from Iraq or Persia,

and next comes an awkward Oriental Jew in the Orthodox knee-breeches, black stockings, long caftan, and big fur cap. Many of the rest are modern, nervous-looking types such as one might see in any European or American city. Here old and new, East and West, are strangely blended; here is the eternal Jew, in all the forms he has acquired in the two thousand years of the Dispersal when he took on the patterns of his varying environment, returned to his ancient homeland in order to become one nation again at the happy end of an incredibly long tragedy.

On that May 14th the flowers and the people were not alone in giving colour to Tel Aviv. Fluttering from balconies and roof-tops as far as the eye could see was the blue-and-white flag with the Star of David. Shop-windows were draped with flags and they flew from all the street stalls. As always, the pavements were crowded, and an endless stream of cars sped along the roads. It was obvious that some happy occasion was about to be celebrated.

Only a few days earlier the city had reverberated with the thunder of gunfire and explosions from the front at Jaffa, for Tel Aviv lay on the edge of a battlefield. An open road runs from a minaret in Jaffa through the long, straight Yarkon Street into Allenby Street, the main thoroughfare of Tel Aviv, and Arab sharpshooters at the top of the minaret had found excellent targets on the shoppers there, some of whom had paid for their carelessness with their lives. Then Jewish troops had advanced to the attack and a bitter struggle had been fought for Jaffa. Ancient hostility between the two towns had broken out afresh.

If Tel Aviv is new, Jaffa, on the other hand, is a thousand years old and its origins are lost in antiquity. Legend says that it was on the rock at Jaffa that Andromeda lay in chains until Perseus freed her. There are references in both the Old and the New Testament to Jafo—which means 'the fair one'—and the place was also known as Joppa. It was here that Jonah embarked on the adventurous voyage which ended in the belly of the whale; and it was here, too, on the flat roof of Simeon the Tanner's house, that the apostle Peter saw his vision of the clean and unclean animals which inspired him to baptize the first gentiles.

At the start of Jewish immigration into Palestine, towards the close of the nineteenth century, many Jews settled in Jaffa. Accustomed for generations to an urban life, they set up there as small tradesmen and artisans, as their forebears had done in the ghettos. But they could never feel anything but foreigners in this Arab town, and so, at the beginning of this century, they resolved to build what was then thought of as a garden suburb, to which they could move out and in it create their own environment. They chose the Hebrew name of Tel Aviv, which means something like 'Spring Hill'; in their metaphorical tongue they called it 'the mount of the sprouting corn'. The coat of arms incorporated a gate over waves, to symbolize a city on the sea and a gateway for the people of the Dispersal to their old home. As Jewish immigration increased, Tel Aviv rapidly expanded and had soon overtaken its Arab parent. Then, in that fateful year 1948, the two cities clashed in battle and whole districts were blasted by gunfire; scarred walls and ruins tell the tale of those grim months, to this day.

The fighting, however, was now at an end and Jaffa in Jewish hands. Suddenly, as the city surrendered, most of its 60,000 inhabitants had fled. Jewish soldiers stood on guard at the street corners against possible surprises; outside an abandoned cinema flapped what remained of the last poster, which advertised *Gone with the Wind*.

Superficially, Tel Aviv resembled a fashionable resort on the Riviera or the Florida coast. Who would have thought that it was on the brink of a far more menacing war than the one that had just ended in victory, and that at any moment hostile aircraft might rain their bombs upon it? Cars were speeding along the roads, shop-windows displayed choice goods, long queues stood outside the cinemas, and the strains of *Rhapsody in Blue* or the tango *Jealousy* could be heard drifting from restaurants.

All the same, there was an air of tension. Frequent news

14

bulletins sounded through the open doors of balconies; news-boys ran hither and thither crying their headlines at the pedestrians. Hundreds of young men and women strolled about the streets in temporary uniforms, ready for action. From the large Mugrabi building in the centre of the city loudspeakers announced the year groups that were being called up for immediate service.

Something big was afoot; and while new recruits hurried through the streets or rode off in trucks and buses for unknown destinations, the crowds in the main streets pressed closer in order to see what was about to happen 'somewhere in Tel Aviv'. Taxis and cars were now seen to be going in the direction of Rothschild Boulevard. The faces of their passengers were familiar from the newspapers and public platforms. The nation's leaders all seemed to be going in the same direction. As the crowd followed them, Rothschild Boulevard became thick with people, who were soon rewarded.

Standing outside the white museum of Tel Aviv Jewish troops formed for the first time a guard of honour and presented arms as prominent personages stepped from their cars and entered by the front door. In the not very big central hall inside hung an immense portrait of Theodor Herzl, the founder of Zionism. David Ben-Gurion took his seat beneath it along with the Ministers designate, and surrounded by members of the National Council and invited guests.

An orchestra struck up the *Hatikvah*, the Jewish National Anthem (the name means 'Hope'), and all present joined in singing it. As the last plaintive notes of the anthem died away, Ben-Gurion rose to speak. The eyes of everyone were turned on him as he walked the few steps which led to the improvised rostrum. He lost no time in coming to the point; there were to be no long speeches.

'I have to read Israel's declaration of independence.'

And as the assembled audience and tens of thousands of listeners all over the country hung on his words, he read out the long proclamation.

The gist of the declaration is that 'Israel bases herself on the doctrines of freedom, justice, and peace, as taught us by the Hebrew prophets; she will establish full social and political equality for all her citizens regardless of race, creed, or sex; she will protect the sublime and sacred shrines and sanctuaries of all religions; and she will adhere to the principles set forth in the Charter of the United Nations.' The declaration ends: 'Trusting in Almighty God, we sign this declaration at this assembly of the Provisional Council of State in the city of Tel Aviv on this day, Friday the fifth *iyar* of the year 5707 after the Creation.'

One by one the thirty-seven members of the National Council went up to the table and signed the document.

Then once more the *Hatikvah* rang out, this time as a hymn of thanksgiving. Old Rabbi Maimon of Jerusalem, the Minister of Religions, now mounted the rostrum, his prayer mat over his head, and, with the tears rolling down his cheeks, read the great prayer of thanksgiving, the *Shehekejanu*: 'Praise be to God, who hath brought us to this day.' And the assembly responded with a deep 'Amen', like a congregation in church.

It was morning over Jewry. The State of Israel had been born. A light extinguished for nearly two thousand years had been relit.

A Russian historian has said that the Slavs have no history, only geography. With the Jews it is the other way round: they have plenty of history but no geography. Roaming the world for thousands of years they never forgot Zion. Yearly at the Passover the exiles would greet one another with '*Leshanah habah be-Jerushalajim*' ('Next year in Jerusalem'), and even in the Dispersal the Law required them to celebrate the wine harvest in the lost homeland. This was what Disraeli meant when he said that people who continued to celebrate the wine harvest when there were no grapes would one day regain their vineyard.

Wherever the Jew wandered his thoughts were fixed on the land he could never hope to see. Then, at long last, miracles began to occur: the lost land was regained.

In the long history of man the release of the people of Israel from their bondage in Egypt has stood out as the great example of liberation from slavery; the parting of the Red Sea has brought hope to many despairing breasts. A similar sense of wonder is associated with the modern birth of Israel. Doubt and despair were conquered by faith and hope. The Jewish people gave the world a new gift.

'And the evening and the morning were the first day.' Six times in the first chapter of Genesis, after each act of the Creation, these words are repeated. '*Vajhi erev vajhi boker,*' it says in the Hebrew: 'And it was evening, and it was morning.'

It may be wondered why the evening should come first, since in the West we begin our reckoning with the morning; but in the Orient the day begins at sunset with the appearance of the first stars, and the Bible, having been written in the East, was of course influenced by Eastern thought.

In this mode of reckoning there may be some hidden wisdom. At least, only those who have known darkness can appreciate the light.

The history of the Jewish people followed the same pattern as the Biblical manner of reckoning: first there was the evening, then the morning. For sixty generations intense darkness enveloped the people of Israel; generation after generation hoped, prayed, and longed for the sunrise, but night seemed never-ending.

The day has dawned only in our lifetime; and as the night can seem darkest just before daybreak, so also in this case: only those who experienced the night can know how black it was. Before we survey the new-won land and Israel's achievement, we must go with her through the valley of the shadow of death and the darkness of night. We must go back to Hitler's Germany and behind the Iron Curtain. When we have done that we shall see the road which leads to the new Israel.

It was evening, and it was morning.

II

THE FINAL SOLUTION

❦

T HE house I was looking for was still there; remarkably
enough, because the district where it stood had been laid
waste. The place was the Kurfürstenstrasse in Berlin; not
the fashionable Kurfürstendamm, but the similarly named
street which runs due east. The city hereabouts had been
blasted in British air raids towards the end of the war and was
overgrown with weeds. A smoke-blackened ruin over to the
west was all that remained of the Kaiser Wilhelm Gedächtnis-
kirche. When hundreds of bombers had dropped their deadly
fire bombs one night in November 1943 the church had been
a pillar of flames; the clock still stood as 2.32, the moment
when the works had melted and time had stopped for the garish
memorial to an Empire that was already a thing of the past.
The golden angel on the top of the Sieges-Säule to the north
glittered in the sunshine; it had crashed the same night but
had been restored.

This was once *Der alte Westen*, the fashionable quarter of
Berlin, conveniently close to the Tiergarten and Zoo, and con-
sisting of grandiose villas and over-blown blocks of expensive
flats with stiff pastiches of classical figures in period stucco.
On that November night the whole area had been a raging sea
of fire. Even the vast air-raid shelter had been smashed and
hundreds of people killed in its ruins.

The taxi-driver had given me a look of surprise when I had
asked him to take me to Kurfürstenstrasse, No. 116.

'Was wollen Sie da? Dort is alles kaput,' he had said. 'What do
you want there? It's all wiped out.'

But I had come to Berlin especially to see if this house was still there, and I insisted on going. Shaking his head, he started up the taxi and we drove off into the wastes. And there, in the distance, I saw the grey silhouette of a solitary house still standing in the shattered street. It was like an old man's smile when it reveals a single tooth protruding from a bare gum.

'Stop over there,' I said.

I looked about eagerly for the number. Sure enough, there it was. Quickly I paid off the taxi and began an inspection.

Those who built the house, many decades ago, must have built well. The bombs had knocked holes in it and it had been on fire. But it still stood—the only building in the district that had survived. It was almost empty now. In a corner of the ground floor opening on to the street there was a *Bierstube*, and under the roof a war invalid lived with his family. That was all. There were six storeys, with fine windows and elegant stone figures on the frontage. Entering through the portico, I found myself in a courtyard in which tall elm trees were making a vain attempt to get at the sun. Though scorched by the flames, they spread a canopy over the courtyard. The steps leading to the main entrance were broad and marble-faced. The place had once been smart and fashionable.

Proceeding from storey to storey and inspecting every corner of the house, I could understand why so much had been spent on it. The house had been a Jewish lodge—*Jüdisches Brüder-vereinshaus*. There had been assembly halls and smaller meeting rooms, as in any Freemasons' lodge, and there were remains of fittings and symbols which only the initiated would have appreciated. Of course there had been a restaurant, complete with huge kitchens, and also a couple of storeys set aside for large dwellings.

It is a small world. When, in a *kibbutz* in Galilee, I happened to mention that I had been in this lodge, one of the inhabitants, a miraculous survivor of Berlin's Jewry, exclaimed:

'My parents were married there.'

It is a long time now since the Jews of Berlin held gay celebrations in that house, and some very different events occurred there before the bombs rained down on Berlin, leaving the house half a ruin. For a glimpse of those events we must go back twenty years.

The black-and-white swastika flew over the entrance, indicating that the house had been taken over by the State. As it was Jewish the Government had confiscated it, and it had been turned into the headquarters of Bureau IVA, 4b, under RSHA. During the Second World War this jumble of figures and letters had concealed the identity of a vast organization which had spread like a giant spider's web over most of Europe.

Two black-uniformed soldiers with sub-machine guns under their arms checked the passes of those who went in and out. These were SS men, members of Hitler's pretorian guard.

'SS' stood for *Schutzstaffel*, or Defence Corps. At the start Hitler had formed the SA stormtroops, the Brownshirts, a paramilitary body of men always spoiling for a fight. The SS, superimposed on this mass organization in 1925, were picked men who had undergone special training and were subject to an iron discipline. Holding police and military powers, they were the instruments of Nazi terrorism in Germany and later the occupied countries.

The power of a totalitarian State rests on the police, and in Germany this was responsible to the SS. The ordinary police were insufficient for the tasks, and more important bodies were the SD, the *Sicherheitsdienst* (or Security Service), and the SP, or *Sicherheitspolizei* (Security Police). These were the régime's eyes and ears, busy in every corner of the Reich. At the outbreak of war in September 1939 all these police services were combined under the RSHA, or *Reichssicherheitshauptamt* (Headquarters, Reich Security). It was a ring of iron encompassing the most ruthless police State the world had ever known. The RSHA was divided, with German thoroughness, into seven *Amtsgruppen* (Departments). Department IV was the Gestapo, or Secret State Police. Section A of this was concerned with internal German affairs, and sub-section 4 was responsible for religious matters. This was subdivided in its turn: sub-section b dealt with the Jews.

It follows that RSHA IVA, 4b was the means available to Hitler for carrying out his resolve to exterminate the Jews. This was the sinister office I had succeeded in finding.

At 7.30 every morning as punctually as clockwork a black Mercedes car drove through the gateway of Kurfürstenstrasse No. 116. As the sentries saluted stiffly, a man sprang out of the car, absently returned the salute, and strode up the steps into his office. But for the uniform, he could have been a grocer's assistant. He was a slim, black-haired man in his forties whose features might have been Jewish. This man was *Obersturmbannführer* Karl Adolf Ecihmann, head of RSHA IVA, 4b.

There was nothing extraordinary about Eichmann; no brilliant personal qualities to mark him out from birth for the influence and power that were to exceed those of a grand inquisitor. Like most of the top Nazis, Eichmann was an ordinary timid little man, the sort that would have been lost in a crowd. He might have spent his days unnoticed as a lowly clerk, but for an evil fate which made him a tool in the hands of sinister men who ruled most of Europe and whose greatest crime was the genocide of the Jews. For this one reason Eichmann entered the limelight and has now found his macabre place in Jewish history.

Of course legends have been built up around the character of Eichmann. According to one of them, he was born in Palestine, in the German settlement of Sarona near Tel Aviv. In fact, he was born, in 1906, in the German town of Solingen, but spent his childhood at Linz in Austria, the city where, some twenty years earlier, the boy Adolf Hitler grew up. Eichmann's father had meant him to go to a university, but his plans were thwarted by the inflation. Finding himself suddenly ruined, young Eichmann had to be content with the agency of an oil firm. Like other disappointed men, he took to Nazism and crossed into the promised land of Germany, where in time he rose to the rank of sergeant of the SS and was posted to SD headquarters in Berlin. His job there was to keep the files of Freemasons' lodges, in offices that were shared at that time with the department of Zionist affairs. These somehow attracted

Eichmann's interest. Possibly it was a defence mechanism against his colleagues' banter about his Semitic features; at any rate, he began to study Yiddish and Hebrew and soon was regarded as the SD's expert on Jewry.

That was the start, and in time the sergeant had risen to the rank of *Obersturmbannführer*, equal to that of a lieutenant-colonel, and was head of the RSHA IVA, 4b. In this post he wielded special powers, was responsible only to Reinhardt Heydrich, the head of the Gestapo, and had direct access to the all-powerful *SS-Reichsführer* Heinrich Himmler himself, nick-named Reichsheini. These three names—Eichmann, Heydrich, and Himmler—are the signatures on the death sentence that was pronounced on the Jews.

But the counter-signature was that of Adolf Hitler himself. And we will now turn to the years in which Hitler and his men evolved and ruthlessly carried out what in Nazi terminology they called *Die Endlösung der jüdischen Frage* (The Final Solution of the Jewish Problem). To pick up the threads of this tangled web we must go back to the 1920s.

Berlin between the wars was a drab and ugly waste of stone set in the middle of the Brandenburg plain, its millions of inhabitants crowded together in tenements. But nature had not been strangled altogether and one of the open spaces was the blue Havel lake with the pine woods of Grunewald by its shores. Here, during the Empire and the Weimar Republic, a fashionable quarter had grown up, with palatial villas and artificial lakes laid out in parks. One of the finest of these, a fastidiously furnished house, belonged to Walther Rathenau, in 1922 the Minister of Foreign Affairs.

On a summer's day in that year—it was actually Midsummer Day—Rathenau was travelling into the city centre in his open car. He would arrive with his usual punctuality at the Ministry at 11 o'clock sharp. At the point where the Königsallee, the main road which ran through the Grunewald, made an S-bend, the chauffeur as usual slowed down. At that moment another car, which had been following the Minister's, drove up alongside.

Two men in leather jackets and hoods stood up in the rear. Then at point-blank range one of them fired a machine gun at Rathenau and the other flung a hand grenade. Seeing the Minister drop dying from his seat, the driver of the other car increased his speed and drove off. The two assassins had changed the course of German history, and with it the history of the world and of Jewry.

They had carried out the orders of one of the terrorist organizations—in this case the Ehrardt Brigade—which had harassed Germany in the years of her defeat. There was fertile soil for them. Under the pressure of war debts, reparations, and territorial losses, the economy had broken down. The middle classes, the white-coated class, and the working man stared poverty and starvation in the face. In desperation many Germans began to turn their eyes to the east and set their hopes on the Socialist experiment that was being made by the new Soviet Russia. The figure of Karl Marx had risen and cast its shadow menacingly over trusts and banks.

There were other forces at work in Germany. *Der Kaiser ging, die Generäle blieben* (The Kaiser went, the generals remained). The Kaiser had barely crossed the border into Holland when the new Social-Democratic Government called on the generals to maintain law and order. They did so with an iron hand. The Spartacus revolt and the violent attempt to turn Bavaria into a Communist State were crushed. But as a result reactionary elements—nationalists, junkers, industrial magnates, and merchant princes—gained the upper hand in the new Weimar Republic. The *Herrenklub*—the Thyssens, Hugenbergs, and von Papens—were in control.

For the menace of Russian Communism the frightened magnates had only one solution: the erection of a bulwark against Bolshevism. Those classes who were attracted by the siren strains of Russia must be educated—by fair means or foul—into regarding the red flag and all it stood for as their worst enemies.

It was foul means; for every conceivable form of terror was let loose. A secret Westphalian court, *Das Fehmgericht*, was resurrected in the best Ku-Klux-Klan style; *Wehrwolfgruppen*

(Werewolves) stalked the land; the Ehrardt and other para-military organizations, springing up like mushrooms, launched a guerilla campaign of ambushes and assassinations. They had terrifyingly free hands. Between 1919 and 1922 there were 376 political murders in Germany. Left-wingers were guilty of twenty-two of them; the other side were responsible for the rest. Nearly all the latter escaped, while eighteen of the former were sentenced, ten to death.

Nearly half of the population of Germany—forty-eight per cent in 1932—belonged to the lower middle classes, Das Kleinbürgertum. They were tradesmen, clerks, artisans, shop workers, smallholders. They bore the main burden of defeat, depression, and inflation; its straps bit deep into their flesh. They found themselves between the Devil and the deep blue sea, ground between the mills of big capital and the consolidated organizations of the workers. They were impoverished, dishonoured, and robbed of their Empire. They thirsted for a faith; they had no religion.

But there was one that could be given to them; namely, anti-Semitism. In this they could find all that they needed, notably a feeling of superiority; for were they not the chosen people, the noblest creation of God, the Aryan race? A religion must have ritual, and that was amply provided, in the form of banners, processions, inspiring songs, and symbols that set the the heart aglow. Orators called upon them to look out across the bleeding frontiers to provinces that had been wrested from them and were now to be re-won. The prospect of a brilliant future was held out, with bread, work, and glory for the chosen people. The new religion also made its demands, calling for sacrifices, discipline, blind obedience. Besides a god, a religion must also have a devil. All the evil, poverty, disappointments, and failures of the Aryan race came from one source—the Jews. They were to be implacably hated.

It is an old story, which has left a trail of blood across two thousand years of Western history. Often in the past when disaster overtook a nation or a city the Jews were blamed for it. They set fire to the cities, poisoned the wells, conspired with the enemy, instigated revolutions, caused falls on the stock exchange. And who was to blame for the present disasters? Of course the Jews. They had stabbed the unbeaten German army in the back. From where had Bolshevism come? From the Jews. The Spartacist, Rosa Luxemburg, Kurt Eisner, the man behind the Bavarian revolution, Bela Kun (Berle Cohen), the butcher of Hungary, were not all these Jews?

The Jew made an excellent scapegoat. The French, the British, the Poles were unassailable; they were conquerors, armed to the teeth, with their feet on Germany's neck. But the Jew was an easy prey, on whom a strong man could exercise his muscles without risk, and perhaps even profit by it financially. It was from this morass that Rathenau's murderers had emerged.

In 1922 Walther Rathenau was a man in his middle fifties. He came of old Berlin Jewish stock, his grandfather having belonged to the circle which met in the *salon* of Rachel Levin. His father, Emil Rathenau, had been a pioneer of modern German industrialism who in 1887 had founded the *Allgemeine Elektricitätsgesellschaft*, the celebrated AEG, which had electrified Germany and in time come to control wide technical and financial interests in Germany and other countries. Walther Rathenau had followed his father's career; but his historical importance was to lie elsewhere. In the First World War he organized the national supplies of raw materials and he joined the Weimar governments after the revolution. He paved the way for a new foreign policy which included the honouring of the Versailles treaty.

Naturally, Rathenau knew what risks he was taking. As a symbol of the new Germany which extended the hand of friendship to Europe, he was, in the eyes of reactionaries, a traitor. What is more, he was a Jew. Nationalist stormtroops sang openly in Upper Silesia:

> *Knallt ab den Walther Rathenau,*
> *die gottverdammte Judensau.*

> Shoot down Walther Rathenau,
> That God-damned Jewish sow.

And so one day in the Grunewald he was cruelly murdered.

'The bullet which killed Rathenau struck all Germany.'
The words were spoken by President Ebert in his memorial speech, and proved to be only too true. Though the murderers were caught and sentenced, it is a sinister fact that the ringleaders were never brought to book. The murder of Rathenau was to be no German Dreyfus affair; no German dared to be a Zola. But there is one human aspect of the tragedy which deserves to be remembered. Rathenau's aged mother, writing to the mother of one of the assassins, said:

'In unutterable sorrow I hold out a hand to you, unhappiest of women. Tell your son that in the name of the murdered man I forgive him, as God also will do, if he confesses and repents . . .'

International reaction to the crime was reflected in plain figures. On June 1, 1922, a dollar was worth 273 marks; a fortnight after the murder its value was 527 marks. *Wie steht der Dollar?* (How does the dollar stand?) became a common newspaper heading. A year later the dollar was worth two-and-a-half trillion marks. Those were the days when the tragi-comic story was told of the three men—an Englishman, a Frenchman, and a German—who lunched together at a restaurant. The Englishman paid his bill with a sovereign, the Frenchman with a pile of notes; while the German handed to the waiter a heavy, square parcel. The parcel contained the blocks for printing currency notes, to enable the waiter to make as many as he wanted.

From the day Rathenau was torn from his rescuing operation Germany was bankrupt. The world depression of 1929 only set the seal on what had been decided, in the case of Germany, seven years earlier. Out of the jungle of terrorism and anti-Semitism emerged the Nazi movement which was to overwhelm a puzzled and perplexed people. Hitler took possession of the vacant throne of Germany. With the opening of the first Nazi Reichstag the cry went out over the streets of the capital:

Deutschland erwache, Juda verrecke!
Germany, awake; perish Judah!

On a foggy day in December, a week or so before the old year would die, I found a rose blooming in my garden. The pale flower, appearing so unexpectedly in the wintry gloom, seemed to me then more lovely than all the roses of summer. So with the Jews, who just before the catastrophe which overwhelmed them experienced a late flowering that surprised the world.

In no other country had assimilation gone so far as it had in Germany. Most Jews there had done all they could to be German. They had given evidence of it in the First World War. More than in any other country, the Jews of Germany had joined up with enthusiasm. A hundred thousand had served in the armed forces—nearly a fifth of the Jewish population. Ten thousand of them fell and 35,000 were decorated for bravery. But they failed to observe that in the middle of the war the Prussian Minister for War had ordered a census of Jews at and behind the front. It was the old lurking suspicion that they would lie low till the storm was over.

At the end of the war the Jews looked forward to the future with rosy optimism. President Wilson had promised a world that would be safe for democracy. Everything boded well. The young Republic granted the Jews equal rights with other citizens and admitted them to public offices, schools, and universities. Side by side with other Germans, the Jews took a hand in restoring the country. Of the 423 delegates at Weimar who drafted the new German constitution six were Jews, and its actual author was a Jewish professor of law, Hugo Preuss. Hugo Haase, founder of the Independent Socialist Party, and Otto Landsberg were among the six Socialists of the provisional Government which steered the ship of State through the first stormy months after the Armistice. In the *Berliner Tageblatt*, Theodor Wolff supported the Democratic Party, whose chief representative was Walther Rathenau.

The new civil liberties encouraged a lively activity in every branch of science and art. Astonished visitors from abroad saw a resurgence of the German theatre, the emergence of Expressionism in painting and sculpture, the development of modern architecture, new trends in music, literature, and journalism.

And by one of those inexplicable whims of fate, a disproportionate number of the artists and scientists were Jews or half-Jews. Of 38 winners of Nobel prizes 11 were Jews. Of Prussia's 28,982 medical men in 1924, 4505, or 15.5 per cent, were Jews; of 9559 lawyers, 2239, or 26 per cent. In the 1920s in Berlin alone there were more practising Jewish lawyers than there were non-Jewish. I have listed the Jewish intellectuals in Imperial and Republican Germany in another book. Let me merely add that in the final, strained weeks before the outbreak of war in 1914 the German and British Governments delegated two of their leading Jews, Albert Ballin and Sir Ernest Cassel, for a secret conference, hoping that 'brothers in blood' would find a solution to the dispute and avert a conflict. In the heat of battle Germany put out her first secret peace feelers through Zionist organizations. When these facts became known later on they provided Hitler with a pretext for accusations against 'international Jewry'.

All this is common knowledge, though perhaps not fully appreciated. The Jewish contribution to modern civilization has been a large and varied one. But many of those who made it were in no way conscious of their Jewishness; some of them, indeed, strove to forget it and became more or less assimilated. It was the scourge of Hitlerism that was to rouse them to its realization. All the same, there were German Jews who had no need of such shock treatment because they had always known they were Jews and been proud of it; and it was this primal Jewry that in the last decades before the deluge blossomed forth anew. Two names are outstanding among many.

Leo Baeck was, from 1912, a Berlin rabbi. An existentialist of Judaism, one might call him. Wittily and warmly, in print and from the pulpit, he preached his theology of moral perfection. As Baeck saw it, Judaism was the classical religion of action, as Christianity was the religion of emotion. In the critical 1920s and 1930s he was the undisputed central figure among German rabbis. So great was his reputation that it impressed even the top Nazis. At any rate, they offered as late as 1938 to allow him to leave the country. Baeck, however, refused. He would remain at his post, sharing the bad and the good with the community which he served. Afterwards, for five long years in the hell of Theresienstadt, he embodied the faith which he had preached, inspiring thousands with the strength to survive or—for most of them—to die well.

Martin Buber had been born in Vienna but studied at universities in Germany. For many years he had been professor of Jewish religious philosophy at Frankfurt am Main, the old centre of Jewish culture in Germany. Because he had been greatly interested in Zionism since early youth, it was natural that, in his sixties, he should leave to become a professor at the Hebrew University of Jerusalem. It was through Polish Jewry that Buber became known. Outward forms had no meaning for him, but only the inner life, such as he found it expressed in Polish Hasidism. It was on this foundation that he based his own neo-mysticism, whereby faith is declared through a dualogue between God and man—Buber's 'I-Thou' relationship. Incidentally, they were ideas which had no small influence on contemporary Christian theology. A man, says Buber, first finds himself when he learns to say 'Thou' to God. There is one other thing. As Buber puts it:

'You know that you need God more than you need anything else. But do you know that God needs you no less?'

An almost pathetic example of an assimilated Jew who 'returned home' was Franz Rosenzweig, whose career was typical of that of a number of Jews of his time. Rosenzweig realized in his early twenties that the old faith had lost its vitality; he saw it as a barren system of rules and precepts. So he resolved to abandon the appearance also and be baptized as a Protestant Christian. But—he said to himself—if I am to be a Christian—I will enter the Church in the same way as most Christians do—though in my case as a Jew. So during the weeks preceding the arranged baptism he regularly attended services in the synagogue. It so happened that the last of these fell on the eve of *Yom Kippur*, 'the Day of Atonement', and Rosenzweig was so moved by the stirring *Kol Nidre* service that when he left the synagogue his decision to become a Christian had crumbled. On its ruins a fresh resolve was born: he would take his stand on the heritage of his ancestors that he had been about to reject.

Rosenzweig began to study Yiddish and Hebrew and to read the Jewish classics. Serving as a German NCO in Poland during the First World War, he made close contact with the vigorous primal Jewry of Poland, which he was to regard for the rest of his life as a measure of the true spiritual life. Beside it most of the stunted Judaism of the West seemed pale.

Rosenzweig died in 1929, at the early age of forty-three. By then he was completely paralysed by the sclerosis from which he had suffered. But though helpless physically, he had the strength of spirit to complete a vast amount of literary work; tied to his chair, his head supported by a cushion, he dictated articles and letters to his wife. Visitors to his house were rewarded with the sight of a rare victory of mind over matter. Rosenzweig succeeded in developing his philosophy, which is a synthesis of faith and reason by which modern Jews can live and die. Most had more use for the latter.

Way back in 1909 Adolf Hitler, aged twenty at the time, read an obscure little journal called *Ostara*, which appeared in Vienna where he lived. The paper was written and published by a former Cistercian monk, one Dr Lanz von Liebenfels, who had founded what he called 'The Order of the New Temple'. This mysterious enterprise had its headquarters in the castle of Werfenstein on the Danube, where it flew a red swastika flag. The facts about Liebenfels are also obscure and it has only recently been realized what an arsenal of ideas he must have been to the Nazi chief.

Liebenfels has told the story of how, one day in 1909, he received a visit at his office by Hitler. It was in the latter's poverty-stricken youth, when, not having the money to take a tram, he had walked all the way from Vienna. Hitler related how he had bought *Ostara* at a newsagent's in the Felberstrasse where he lived and how he had been fascinated by its contents.

There were a few numbers which he wanted, he said, in order to complete the set. Sorry for the shabby-looking youth, Liebenfels gave him the papers, together with his return fare.

In *Ostara* the rudiments of the Hitlerite doctrines may be found. In it Liebenfels expounds his racial ideas about fostering a patrician caste, blond and blue-eyed, predestined to rule over the ape-men: the dark, hook-nosed Jews. For these inferior creatures he advocates drastic measures such as castration, sterilization, forced labour, deportation, liquidation. Long passages of *Mein Kampf* were lifted straight out of *Ostara*. Not unfairly, Liebenfels has been called 'the man who gave Hitler his ideas'. Hitler, of course, displayed no gratitude to his teacher, but, fearing that his plagiary might be found out, had *Ostara* banned and forbade Liebenfels either to write or to publish anything else.

History has its bitter ironies, and one of these is the suggestion that Hitler himself may have been quarter-Jewish. Certain it is that his father's mother, Maria Anna Schicklgruber, 'got herself into trouble' while in the service of the Jewish family of Frankenberger, and that the son is suspected of having been the father of the boy Alois to whom she gave birth in 1837. It is a fact that for years she received financial assistance from the Frankenbergers. Alois Schicklgruber changed his name to Hitler and in his third marriage fathered Germany's Führer-to-be. If this story is true Hitler would have been subject to his own anti-Jewish laws.

It is possible that he got wind of his grandmother's serious slip later in life; there are indications that he may have done. But during his youth he had no inkling of it and the Jews meant nothing to him. In Linz, where his family lived when he was a boy, there were practically no Jews; he himself said that he could not recall ever having heard the word 'Jew' during his childhood. But in Vienna, where he arrived as a young man, he found himself in a sea of anti-Semitism, with Liebenfels only one among many. It is possible that personal factors lit the fuse. The penniless painter strove in vain to sell the products of his slender talent. Idle and restless, he wasted his days among the dregs of the capital, barely keeping body and soul together. There may have been a clash with a Jew; a native jealousy; or a sense of inferiority. Whatever the cause, in those years he developed a wholly insane hatred of the Jews. It was to remain the most lasting and most persistent element in his ideas; his whole character and later development were dominated by it. One quotation from *Mein Kampf* will suffice:

'Is there any underhand activity, any depravity, particularly in cultural matters, where at least one Jew is not involved? Cut such an abscess and there straightway appears, like the maggot in a rotten carcase, a little Jew, dazzled by the light of day.'

Hitler's whole abnormal character sheds its sinister light on his anti-Semitism. There was something rather dubious about the sexual life of his early years. Conditions in the Hitler home were so cramped that incest is not far to seek. In his late twenties he lived with the daughter of his sister, Geli Rauval. The relationship ended abruptly and cruelly when the girl was found shot. It might have been suicide, but it looked more like the hand of an unknown avenger. The love affair and its ending produced in Hitler one of his periodic bouts of depression. There is no wonder that his hatred of the Jews took on a tinge of morbid sexuality. Here is an example of his typical outbursts:

'The swarthy Jew, with diabolical glee depicted on his face, lies in wait for the unsuspecting girl, whom he defiles with his blood.'

On another occasion he speaks of a nocturnal vision, like a nightmare, in which hundreds of thousands of girls are seduced by repulsive, hook-nosed Jews.

These ideas of *Rassenschande* (race pollution) found free vent in the pornographic sheet *Der Stürmer*.

There were mysteries in the mind of Hitler which only an acute psychologist could fathom. One can only suppose that his hatred of the Jews began as a form of self-hatred, and that

Tel Aviv from the air

The Dan Hotel at Tel Aviv

The last ghetto
fighters in Warsaw

~ Diese Banditen verteidigten sich mit der Waffe. ~

Before the massacre

—and after

it ended as a cloak for personal problems he was incapable of solving. If such was the case, he was not the first to have projected his guilt feelings on to the Jews.

The hideous fact is that those obscure impulses controlled and governed a modern Machiavelli, one to whom good and evil, truth and lies, promises and perjuries, all could be used, provided that they led him to the desired objective. On top of this there was Hitler's remarkable sense of propaganda. Unfailingly he was able to find weapons in the boundless arsenal of anti-Semitism. Anti-Semitism has flourished in Germany for centuries and after the war it broke out as never before. Seizing the opportunity, Hitler fed the German people with all its theories and prejudices and they swallowed them whole, to an extent that was beyond belief. The Jew was called the 'November criminal', the traitor, the Bolshevik, the secret international foe, the Freemason in league with world capital, even with the leaders of the Churches. He was the root cause of all that excluded Germany from her natural markets and from an influence on world affairs. Every day the Jew distilled a poison that was worse than the plague, the poison of Bolshevism. And this was synonymous with all that his audiences could not endure: pacifism, nudism, jazz, the abolition of capital letters, Chaplin films, functionalistic architecture, Expressionist painting, Reinhardt's theatre productions, psycho-analysis. . . .

The Nazi programme in its full implications can be read in *Mein Kampf*; nothing is concealed there. But no one ever believed that there was a serious chance of its realization; the world had shaken its head and dismissed it as nonsense. Yet in the event no programme has been realized so ruthlessly and so literally.

Hitler was barely in office before it began. In the weeks following the seizure of power the brown battalions filled the streets and took over their newly won Reich. With glee they coshed anyone who looked Jewish; they boycotted Jewish shops, stuck placards on the windows, and posted pickets at the doors. A new law prohibited Jews from holding public office; Jewish children were excluded from publicly maintained schools; Jews were banned from universities, sports clubs, journalism, broadcasting, the stage, and filming; Jewish doctors and dentists were deprived of their practices; Jewish books were publicly burnt. The persecution was carried to grotesque extremes. For example, a Jewish farmer might not take his cow to an Aryan's bull and veterinary surgeons refused to trim Jewish dogs. Jews were not allowed to play Bach, Beethoven, or Mozart.

The whole culminated for the time being in the Nuremberg Laws of September 15, 1935, which deprived Jews of their German nationality. They now ceased to be *Reichsbürger* and became *Staatsangehörige*: second-class citizens whose only 'right' was obedience to the State. The law to 'protect German blood and honour', together with a series of decrees, ensured that the two groups were segregated. Regulations defined full Jews and *Mischlinge* (mixtures)—that is, half-, quarter-, and eight-part Jews—and their status. From then on it paid a German to have an Aryan certificate. Soon every Jewish man was ordered to call himself Israel and every Jewish woman had to take the name of Sarah. The laboriously won emancipation was thus swiftly wiped out; the ghetto had been reintroduced.

The next operation was the *Krystal*, or Crystal, Night of November 9 and 10, 1938. A strange interplay of chance paved the way for it. Since the First World War, a few thousand Jewish refugees from Poland had been allowed to live in Germany. These *Ostjuden*—Eastern Jews—were well settled and many of them had never bothered to get their papers in order. Suddenly, the government in Berlin ordered the deportation of 15,000 of them to Poland. So under police guard they were driven off in sealed cattle trucks to the frontier station of Sbonszyn, where the police began to shepherd them across the border. There, however, they were stopped by Polish frontier guards. Thus they found themselves in no-man's-land under the open sky, with the Gestapo behind them and Polish machine guns in front. There they waited for weeks while the two Governments negotiated about their fate.

A married couple in the party succeeded in sending a post-card to their son, Herschel Grünspan, who lived illegally with an uncle in Paris. When this seventeen-year-old youth read the heart-rending message from his parents, something clicked in him. He bought a pistol, and going to the German Embassy shot the first man he saw, a secretary by name Ernst vom Rath. Two days later vom Rath died of his wounds. This was the spark which exploded the powder-barrel.

The killing came at a convenient time for the Nazi leaders. The news of vom Rath's death had scarcely come in before Heydrich had ordered a nation-wide pogrom. The Brownshirts went into action, and on the night of November 10th there were bonfires in every German town. Hundreds of synagogues went up in flames, Jewish homes were raided, Jews were murdered, their shops looted, 30,000 were arrested and consigned to concentration camps. The Crystal Night takes its name from the piles of broken glass which littered the streets.

The nocturnal terror, shocking enough in itself, was followed by yet another bitter attack, when the Government imposed on the Jews a collective fine of a milliard marks and Goering proclaimed that they should 'vanish from the German economy'. By a series of crushing decrees the Jews were forced to dispose of their financial interests at a tenth of their value, when their possessions were not confiscated altogether. They had been 'Aryanized', it was said. Property worth seven milliard marks was lost in this way; world-famous publishing firms like Ullstein and Mosse shared the same fate with factories and other business both large and small.

The Crystal Night was the first—and the last—occasion on which the anti-Jewish measures were carried out so that all could see them. The ill-treatment in concentration camps took place behind closed doors. But on this one occasion the world at large received first-hand accounts of what it meant to be a Jew in Germany. The Press of America, Britain, France, and Scandinavia naturally denounced these monstrous crimes; but the Governments were noticeably reserved, for it was the period of appeasement just after Munich. Only President Roosevelt took action and recalled the United States Ambassador from Berlin; the other Governments decided to regard the pogroms as an internal German affair. But behind the silence there was bitter disillusion; one important consequence of the German action was that the democracies abandoned their hope of an understanding with Germany. A decisive step had been taken towards the war which broke out the following year.

As for the German Jews themselves, they hoped against hope that the storm would blow over. The great majority regarded themselves as Germans. Jews had lived in Germany for sixteen centuries; surely this sudden wave of persecution was just a passing phase. The Jewish community in Berlin even telegraphed to the Chief Rabbi in Great Britain, requesting him to put a stop to protests and the boycott of German goods. Of course this was naïve and unrealistic; but the wish is father to the thought, and Jews have always hoped till the end that all would be well. Slowly, however, their thoughts turned to emigration as at long last they realized that a Jew could not stay in Germany and survive. Between 1933 and 1935 60,000 left the country; and after the Nuremberg Laws the number rose to 200,000. Of course relief organizations were set up, in particular the *Aliyah* youth organization which rescued children and young people and trained them for farming in Palestine. But after the annexation of Austria 400,000 Jews still remained in the Reich.

Emigration is always tragic, but those German Jews who finally decided to go had more than the usual difficulties to face. How were they to get out, and how were they to get visas for other countries?

The latter problem is a modern one; in the past it was easy for political refugees to find asylum. The Spanish Jews fled to Turkey and the Netherlands, the French Huguenots to Western European countries or America. But between the two world wars immigration into America was restricted by the Johnson Act of 1924, and only a minimum of immigrants were allowed into Palestine under the British Mandate. The German Jews found the doors shut on all sides. One is tempted to quote the sarcastic words of Dr Goebbels:

'They call the Jews pioneers of a new culture, geniuses of philosophy and art. But if anybody asks them to have these geniuses, they shut their doors and say "We have no use for them." This strikes me as being the only example in history of people refusing to welcome geniuses.'

If by a miracle a Jewish family obtained visas for the United States or Britain, they faced another barrier; exit visas were required in order to leave Germany. One might have thought that this would have been a matter of course, considering that the Nazis had declared their intention of making Germany *judenrein*—Jew-free, that is. But it was by no means so simple. And this brings us to a curious feature in the Third Reich. To outward appearances it seemed a firmly knit unit. But we know now that there were continual conflicts of interests and personalities behind the scenes and that a good deal of intriguing went on, so that the left hand rarely knew what the right hand was doing. Moreover, Jewish emigration was all the time a disputed issue, some being in favour of it, some against. There was never any agreement until Hitler decreed the 'final solution'—*Die Endlösung*. Even then there were Jews who managed to buy exit visas.

The policy zig-zagged up to the outbreak of war. For a few years after it had seized power the Nazi Government ran offices which organized emigration. For a time Eichmann was in charge of the central office of Jewish emigration in Prague, which was set up immediately after the occupation. Of course the Jews had to forfeit a considerable part of their property in order to get released, but they were allowed to take some of their capital. After the Crystal Night they had to leave everything behind them except the clothes they stood in. To the Nazis it seemed a shrewd move to saddle their neighbours with these impoverished people; they gave colour to the legends about the wandering Jew. But the doors were shut tight when it was realized that the Jews could be a glorious hostage. Down to 1939 they envisaged the possibility of selling them, of granting collective exit permits to a few hundred thousand at a time in return for international loans. The German financial wizard, Dr Hjalmar Schacht, visited London in order to ventilate this incredible project. Then came the war, and the free nations had greater problems to deal with than the German Jews. The net closed around them.

It was in those years that a Jewish mother in Germany named her baby *Niemand*—Nobody. He had been born without rights.

The eighteen-day *Blitzkrieg* against Poland in September 1939 brought the largest and most vigorous Jewish group in the world under Nazi domination. Since the early Middle Ages the Polish Jews had developed a rich and distinctive culture. Numbering more than three millions, they formed ten per cent of the population and as much as twenty five per cent in the cities. Many of the villages were entirely Jewish.

The idea of total genocide had not yet ripened in Hitler's brain. So far he was considering the establishment of a large Jewish reserve in the Lublin district where two rivers, the Vistula and the San, enclosed a convenient area. After the fall of France a year later a new plan arose, that of using the French colony of Madagascar. It was proposed to transport millions of Europeans there, under German control, at the end of the war.

The Polish Jews were soon taught who were the masters. The badge of Jewry, *Der Judenstern*—a six-pointed star—had to be worn on an armlet or elsewhere on the dress, and had also to be displayed on Jewish shops. A rain of decrees followed. Jews were excluded from trains, buses, and trams without special permission; some streets were closed to them; they were not allowed to smoke in the streets, or to use the pavements; they were banned from theatres and cinemas; their children were expelled from schools. It amused the Nazis to cut off their beards or earlocks. Then the Germans instituted two measures which struck at the very foundations of their existence: thousands of Jews were drafted for forced labour, many being confined to labour camps and set to the roughest of work on ditches and canals, in mines and factories. In these camps flogging and other forms of ill-treatment were common and death from starvation brought a welcome relief.

Then, too, the ghetto was reintroduced. All Jews from the country were moved into Warsaw, Lodz, Krakow, and Lublin, where they lived behind walls they had been forced to build themselves. It was convenient for the time when the Jews would be rounded up for their final extermination. These Polish ghettos were to have a tragic and glorious history, as we shall see later.

The war continued, and on June 22, 1940 'the German forces joined with their Rumanian and Finnish allies' and crossed the frontiers of Russia. Operation Barbarossa, 'the crusade against Bolshevism', had begun. The combined armies struck deep into the Soviet Union; the Baltic States, White Russia, the Ukraine, and the Crimea fell into their hands. In the wake of the advancing armies went the *Einsatz gruppen*, detachments of ss men whose officers for months before the attack had been carefully trained for the tasks that awaited them; namely, counter-espionage, security work, the functions of political commissaries, and keeping an eye on the regular army officers. Above all, it was their business to kill. Hitler had estimated that thirty million Russians would have to die in order to make way for an Aryan colonization. The order came for the extermination of inferior races, which meant chiefly Jews.

The same pattern was followed almost everywhere. When a town was occupied the Jews would be ordered to set up a *Judenrath*—that is to say, a Jewish Council. Its sole business was to register the local Jews. With the lists in their hands the ss troops would round up the Jews, herd them on to lorries, and drive off. The passengers would show little sign of fear, having been reassured by statements that they were being taken to 'new Jewish territory'. But a few kilometres outside the town the lorries would come to a halt in a lonely forest or bog, where long, deep trenches would have been dug in advance. The Jews would be hurriedly unloaded, told to undress, and marched in squads to the graves, where they would be ordered to get in and stand with their heads visible above the edge. Then a round of machine-gun fire would crack and the long rows of people would drop in their graves. An engineer who was an eye-witness of one such frightful scene has given this account of it:

'An old woman with snow-white hair was holding a year-old baby in her arms, singing to it while the child clucked with joy. The parents stood watching them with tears in their eyes. The father was holding their ten-year-old son by the hand, talking softly to him, stroking his head, and pointing to the sky; and the boy was fighting back his tears. An ss man counted out twenty persons in the group, including the family, and they were ordered to the grave. A slender, dark-eyed girl pointed to herself as she passed, and whispered to me: "Twenty-three." I looked into the grave. Already it was three parts filled with bodies and I estimate that there must have been a thousand. They lay one on top of the other with the blood from their heads streaming down over their shoulders. A few raised an arm or turned a head, showing they were still alive. The group of whom I have spoken now arrived and stepped in on top of the corpses. They stood waiting, as they softly caressed one another. Then I heard some bursts of gunfire. . . .'

This is one example among thousands. It has been estimated that 800,000 Russian Jews fell into the hands of the Germans and were murdered in this way. The rest succeeded in escaping with the retreating Russian army. The executioners were ss men; but army officers witnessed the murders and did not protest.

The Germans had good reason for choosing Poland as the centre for their new ghettos. The air of the ghetto has always surrounded the Jews of Poland, who for centuries had succeeded in isolating themselves from the outside world. They were different in language, dress, and habits, as well as physical features. And the ancestral culture which they continued to cherish helped to develop those 'Jewish' characteristics of mental agility, pugnacity, passion, and ambition. Scorn and persecution were their inherited lot, and they had developed the ability to look after themselves with the aid of moral courage, faith, and their wits. Now, when the walls of the ghetto closed in on them for the last time, their powers of resistance could be plainly seen.

Three million Polish Jews were so confined. Each of the many new ghettos was a world unto itself, but the one we know most about is the ghetto at Warsaw. Not only was this the biggest, but a group of historians kept a day-to-day account of what went on there. The records which they buried towards the end have since been recovered and studied. 'What we cannot cry out to the world, we are burying in the ground,' one of the reports concludes.

The wall which surrounded the ghetto enclosed a whole district of central Warsaw nearly two kilometres in length and a kilometre and a half wide. This was the original centre of Jewish settlement and the names of its streets are familiar to readers of Yiddish literature and folklore; they were streets which had known both learning and misery, wisdom and poverty. Included in the area was a newer industrial quarter with straight, dreary streets running north of the central railway station; the Posnan-Berlin line intersected the ghetto. Where formerly 150,000 people had lived, the Germans crowded in half a million. The overcrowding became even worse when the Germans afterwards restricted the area. A single-windowed room was considered enough, on the average, for three or four persons. There was insufficient accommodation even for that. The streets were as thick with people as an Oriental market. It was fertile soil for epidemics, of course, and typhus killed off tens of thousands.

Hunger was the worst. The Germans, carefully controlling the supplies, restricted the rations to 800 calories a day, mostly made up of bad potatoes and *ersatz* fat. The inhabitants, reduced to living skeletons, slowly died and were left lying in the street where they fell. Passers-by would cover them with a newspaper, and then the death-cart would take them away. The bodies of those who died in the houses were laid naked on the pavement, their clothes having been taken by the survivors.

'Jews are like that', a German officer explained to visiting journalists on a sight-seeing tour. Sentries, posted at the gates and on the wall itself, fired on anyone who ventured too near. Of course there were no telephone or public transport connections with the world outside, though internal traffic, during the early months, was served by trolley-buses, which bore the sign of David.

The Germans had appointed a *Judenrath* under a *Judenälteste* (Jewish elder) to administer the internal affairs of the ghetto, but the inhabitants naturally regarded such people as quislings, as indeed some of them were. But if they had thoughts of ingratiating themselves with the authorities in their own interests, they were mistaken; for they all came to the same end in the gas chambers. Of course the manpower of the ghetto was exploited. Every morning long columns under German guard would march out through the gates to do slave labour. Inside the walls there were factories, textile mills, tanneries, and workshops for cleaning and repairing German uniforms. The Germans, incidentally, never succeeded in making the isolation complete; brave people managed to slip in and out through sewers and gaps in the wall, carrying smuggled goods. By the same means the ghetto later procured weapons.

The people of the ghetto held out, hoping against hope that in one way or another they would eventually be freed. It is noteworthy that the suicide rate was well below the average. The streets, too, were bright with flowers, which hung from window-boxes where tomatoes and radishes were also grown. Strength was found in Jewish studies. People read the literature of their ancestors, studied the Bible and the Talmud, argued subtle points of Jewish law. There were amateur drama groups, musical societies, symphony orchestras conducted by world-famous conductors, debating societies, study circles, classes in engraving, leather-work, drawing, even cosmetics; small newspapers were improvised and published; and the available books were passed from hand to hand till they were worn to tatters. The books in greatest demand were those on historical subjects, especially ones which dealt with periods that inspired hope, such as the Napoleonic era with its analogies between Napoleon and Hitler, together with Tolstoy's *War and Peace* and descriptions of the German collapse in 1918. Jewish humour, with its irony and satire, was also a comfort. This is an example, found in the Warsaw records:

Mr Churchill asked a Hasidic rabbi his advice about the best way of defeating Hitler, and got the reply:

'There are two ways, one natural and the other miraculous. The natural one would be for a million angels to descend from the sky and overcome him with swords of fire. The miraculous one would be for a million British troops to land in Europe and invade Germany.'

The Warsaw ghetto endured for a bare two years. As its people braved their fate and kept themselves alive, the death factories were being built outside, mainly with labour from the ghettos. In the summer of 1942 the blow fell on the Warsaw ghetto. The *Judenrath* was ordered to announce that the inhabitants were to be 'transferred to new areas of colonization in the east'. Daily SS men marched into the narrow streets and picked out those who were to go, breaking up families, taking children from their parents, separating husbands from their wives. Then the trains rumbled off with their living cargo, though not to a new colony but to a death camp from which none would return.

By the beginning of 1943 there were only 40,000 Jews left in the Warsaw ghetto. They were the people who fought one of the most memorable battles in human history, the revolt of the ghetto against its German masters.

By this time the final act of the tragedy was about to begin. As the German armies froze fast before Moscow and the United States entered the war, Adolf Hitler made his monstrous decision. On January 20, 1942 Heydrich assembled his fourteen closest associates at the headquarters of the international criminal police, Am Grossen Wannsee Nos 56 and 58, and told them the Führer's instructions. So frightful were they that even Heydrich had to paraphrase them. None of those present, however, was left in any doubt as to the meaning of the order. The Jews of Europe were to be eliminated. The energies of the able-bodied among them were to be utilized to the utmost, so that they would die of their own accord and save the trouble of having to kill them. The rest were to be liquidated forthwith; for that was all they were fit for. The gas chambers were about to operate.

This was the final solution of the Jewish problem—*Die Endlösung der jüdischen Frage.* January 20, 1942 put a period to Jewish existence in German-occupied Europe.

The 'death industry' was nothing new to the Nazis. It was one of their favourite ideas that *Gnadentot*—or mercy-killing—should be the lot of those who were 'unfit to live', by which they meant the insane and mentally deficient, incurables, and 'anti-social types', the last-named category including Jews. Incredibly, a number of scientists had placed their services at the Government's disposal for the realization of these ideas and, under the code name 14F13, had 'treated' some 70,000 persons. At a 'sanatorium' the patients were put into an airtight room, which was then filled with carbon monoxide. (Hitler had been gassed in the First World War and had a partiality for this form of killing.) The relatives would receive a brief notification that the patients had died of a stroke or from pneumonia.

After the conference in Berlin the experts of 14F13 were instructed to instal the required appliances in the death camps. Poland was chosen as a convenient place, both because the 3,000,000 Jews there were already assembled in ghettos and because communications with other occupied countries were easy. Under the direction of Bureau IVA, 4b and its chief Eichmann, the transport trains began to move eastwards. In memory of Heydrich, who had been killed by Czech partisans in May 1942, the operation was called Einsatz Reinhardt.

Operation Reinhardt gradually came under the control of Odilo Globocnik, a man of forty who had been born at Trieste of Austrian parentage and was a fanatical Nazi long before the *Anschluss*. Now this jumped-up foreman bricklayer was awarded the post of Gauleiter in Vienna itself. The promotion was short-lived. Globocnik, an alcoholist, got himself involved in a criminal offence concerning the illegal transfer of foreign exchange and had to be dismissed. But Operation Reinhardt needed people of his calibre and Himmler remembered him, pardoned his 'old friend Globb', and made him head of the SS in Poland. The fate of Odilo Globocnik is veiled in mystery, but probably he took his own life after the capitulation; his victims are dead; and his henchmen either committed suicide or went under ground. As a result, what we know of their macabre work is incomplete, though it is enough to enable us to form an impression of what went on in the death camps.

When the train from Prague to Krakow passed Oświecim (in German, Auschwitz), a small town of Upper Silesia in a dreary area west of Krakow, the passengers would gather at the windows on the side facing the town. It was an experience to get a glimpse of the cowls on the crematorium chimneys in the great concentration camp that was springing up there. Auschwitz, with its annexe Birkenau, together with Belsen (in Polish, Belzec), Sobibor, and Treblinka, in Poland, were the major centres of genocide.

On arrival the transports found, greeting them over the entrance gates, the inscription *Arbeit macht frei*—Work makes you free. Hardly had they got inside when the SS men began to sort them out, putting the able-bodied on the left and the ailing on the right. The former were then sent to the labour squads, where they were brutally exploited for as long as they had any strength left, in factories and in mines. For twelve hours they would have to stand at their work and on roll call, on rations which consisted of weak turnip soup, till they became living skeletons. Then, dressed in rags, they would wait their turn for the gas chamber. The life expectancy of such a slave worker was put at two months; but 'a decent worker dies in three months', it was said.

By comparison, the fate that awaited those who were sorted

out to the left was merciful. They got off with *Sonderbehandlung* —special treatment; that is to say, they were marched straight off to the gas chambers. As they undressed and gave up their valuables, the guards would assure them that they were only to be washed and disinfected. They were then herded into the 'bathrooms', as many as possible at a time—men, women, and children—with the result that after the gas had done its work, the dead would be left standing, there being no room for them to fall. When all were dead, the gas would be removed by electric suction and a special squad—a *Sonderkommando*, or *Scheisskommando*, as they called it at Auschwitz—would then move in, wearing gas-masks and rubber boots. They would spray the corpses with water, break the gold fillings from their jaws, and cut off the women's hair for use in the war industry. The bodies would then be hoisted on to wagons by means of hooks and taken to the crematorium. Night and day the flames would rise from its chimneys. 'That's your only way out,' a grinning prison guard had confided in a newly arrived transport.

The first gas chambers were primitive, some of them being converted railway wagons, while others were just large boxes. The carbon monoxide was directed into these through a hose taken from a car or a captured tank. Later the chambers became marvels of technical ingenuity and would consist of bunkers with several storeys under the ground; the bottom one would contain the gas chamber, where a more efficient poison, Cyklon B, an insecticide, would be used, while the crematorium, on a mass scale, would be at the top. At Auschwitz 10,000 cremations a day were achieved.

'This is a glorious part of our history,' Himmler said at a briefing of ss officers. 'But it has never got into print, and never shall.' He had given strict orders that the liquidations should remain a secret, and after each cremation the relevant documents were all destroyed. But he was mistaken when he thought that his evil deeds would never be published.

The great days of the gas chambers were in 1942 and 1943. In 1944 the Red Army broke through into Poland. Globocnik then quickened the pace, and by 1944 the last 80,000 Jews in the ghetto at Lodz had been sent to Auschwitz. Finally, before the Russians arrived the Germans blew up the death factories and destroyed the files; on the mass graves they planted pine trees. The Russians found only incomplete evidence of what had taken place there; but for months a thin mist of ashes hung over the ruins. It was all that was left of the Jews of Poland and Western Europe.

Two kinds of trains passed through Germany and the occupied countries in those years; there were those that were in the time-tables, and those that were not. Not many people saw the latter, for they travelled mostly at night and during the day stood in sidings. These trains consisted of twenty, thirty, or forty cattle trucks coupled together, the doors being barred and bolted on the outside. They might be long on the way—days, perhaps weeks—before they reached their destination. The passengers would be Jews; packed so tightly in each truck that it was impossible to lie down and difficult even to squat. In summer it would be insufferably hot, in winter perishingly cold. But, summer or winter, a Jewish transport could always be recognized by its appalling smell. It was not often they had latrine pails and the passengers would have to stand in their own dirt. Occasion-ally, singing would be heard in the trucks; one of those Jewish songs with words of joy set to a melancholy tune:

> What will we do when the Messiah cometh?
> We shall rejoice when the Messiah cometh.
> David, our king, will dance for us.
> We shall rejoice when the Messiah cometh.

When the trains finally arrived at their destination and the doors were opened, there might be five or six corpses among the passengers; or perhaps a woman would have given birth to a baby.

Night after night, year after year, the transports travelled eastwards, slowly emptying Germany and her vassals of Jews.

Strangely enough, Germany was the last country from which the transports flowed. For a long time Himmler hesitated before he gave the order for large-scale deportations. The German Jews, therefore, had a brief respite, though they did not go unmolested. The star of David was introduced; rations were restricted mainly to potatoes, rye, flour, and skim milk, and were reduced if a gift parcel was received from abroad. There was persistent victimization. For example, a Jewess sold her mother's-milk to a pedriatist without stating her racial origin, and both were severely punished. The year 1942 saw the end of this period of grace. Suddenly, 100,000 German Jews were transported to Poland, where they vanished up the chimneys of the crematoria at Belsen, Maidanik, and Auschwitz. At the close of 1943 Germany was officially declared *judenrein*, or Jew-free. Austria and Czechoslovakia shared the same fate.

Himmler and Eichmann had few scruples about the occupied countries. The Jews of Holland and Belgium were rounded up in large-scale raids and deported to their deaths, Anne Frank and her family being among them; in small countries there were few hiding-places. Eichmann ran into greater difficulties in France. The border between occupied and Vichy France was only a line on the map, and though difficult it was not impossible to cross, while in this respect, at least, Petain resisted German demands. In Norway the Germans succeeded by a surprise move in capturing most of the Jews, who were not very numerous. In Denmark the story had a happy ending, when the Danish people, making common cause with their Jewish fellow-citizens, hid them during the raids of October 1943 and helped most of them to get across to Sweden, where they found asylum. Out of a Jewish population of 6500, only 475 were deported, to Theresienstadt, and most of them survived to return home at the end of the war.

There were other bright spots, too. To the surprise of the world, Rome and Berlin clashed openly on the Jewish question. It is true that the Fascist Government as early as 1938 had followed Hitler's example in introducing anti-Jewish legislation, but it categorically rejected physical measures. Not that Mussolini could claim any credit for this—he would gladly have handed the Italian Jews over to his Axis partner. But there was

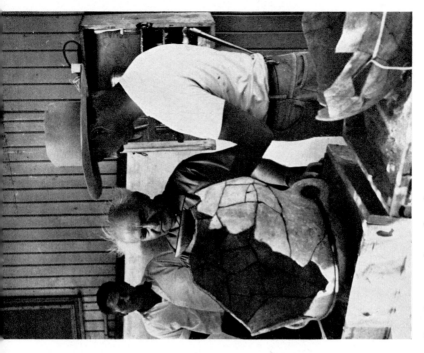

Ben-Gurion and Yigal Yadin

David Ben-Gurion

Excavating at Hazorea

Daily life in the Negev

opposition from the Foreign Ministry and the General Staff, neither of which would be a party to the outrage.

Consequently, there were two places in Europe to which Jews could go—Vichy France and Italy—and a fair number did so. But it was only a temporary asylum; at the end of 1942 the Germans overran the whole of France, and in 1943 they virtually occupied Italy. In Rome alone they rounded up 10,000 Jews whom they carried off to Auschwitz; and though the crime took place outside the Vatican windows, the Pope made no protest.

In south-east Europe fortunes varied. The Bulgarian Government yielded up none of its Jews; but things went badly in Greece, where the old and vigorous Jewish community of Salonika was wiped out. Slovakia and Rumania obeyed their German masters; though, when they saw at last how the war was turning, they began to procrastinate. The rapid advance of the Red Army through Rumania saved half a million Jewish lives. The fate which befell the Jews of Hungary is a separate story.

It was the spring of 1943, with British and American victories in North Africa. The great turning-point of the war had arrived: not the beginning of the end, but the end of the beginning, as Mr Churchill said. It was at this moment, when the free world was beginning to breathe more easily, that things flared up in Warsaw. The last revolt of the ghetto broke out.

As I have said, the isolation of the ghettos was never complete. Down to the end they managed to maintain tenuous contacts with one another. Young men and girls who had blue eyes and fair hair and looked 'Aryan', sometimes even children, would act as couriers, slipping out with their messages through the sewers. In this way they learnt the destination of the transports and the fate of those who went on them; and thus the idea of a last desperate struggle slowly ripened.

It was something new. For thousands of years the one weapon available to the Jews had been passive resistance, though it was not in any way cowardice, as they had demonstrated at Massada, where thousands of men had taken their own lives after first killing their wives and children, just as thousands had died at the hands of the Crusaders and under the Inquisition. When the only alternative was baptism, they chose death.

In Poland now they were up against the most perfect war machine the world had ever seen; and unlike the resistance movements in the occupied countries, the Jews of Warsaw had no hiding-places and were isolated; no friendly planes dropped arms and supplies to them by parachute; no army advanced to their relief, for the nearest front was still 600 miles away. Their only line of retreat would be cellars and sewers. They took up arms, not because they hoped to survive, but because they meant to preserve their honour and dignity and set an example to their fellows.

The core of the Jewish fighting units were the Zionists. Poland had been the principal training-ground of the *halutzim*, the young pioneers who had laid the foundations of the State of Israel in Palestine. While awaiting their turn to emigrate to the promised land they had lived in groups called *kibbutzim*, and they had kept together in the ghetto. Hard physical labour had made them strong and supple; they had a faith and a future. Eichmann called them 'biologically excellent material'. A twenty-four-year-old *halutz*, by name Mordekai Anieliewiecz, assumed the leadership and gathered together a few hundred companions. Their big problem was weapons; all they had to begin with was one pistol. With great labour they managed to smuggle in rifles, pistols, a few machine guns, ammunition, and explosives; but all that most of them had was their bare fists.

April 19th was the Passover and all the bells were ringing for service when the Germans launched their final action to clear the Warsaw ghetto of its last 40,000 inhabitants. Two thousand picked troops with artillery, flame-throwers, and tanks moved in through the gates. The general expected the business to be over in three days. It took thirty-three.

The Jewish fighters were ready waiting. As the Germans

reached the first street they were met by a burst of fire; then young men leapt from their hiding-places and flung Molotov cocktails at the tanks. Two of these went up in flames, the crews with them. The advance stopped as abruptly as it had started.

The Germans realized now that fresh tactics were required. Consequently, Heinkels rained their bombs on the ghetto; the artillery went into action; and flame-throwers sprayed the bombed houses. The ghetto was now in flames and for many nights they formed a landmark over Warsaw. Dreadful scenes took place. There was a mother who appeared at the top of a burning house, holding her two children by the hand; and as the flames licked towards them, she flung the first of the children into the fire, while the other struggled desperately to avoid the same fate. Finally, the woman picked it up and sprang with it into the flames. Everywhere there was a smell of burning flesh.

The destruction of the ghetto did not settle the issue; the brave survivors carried on the battle from shelters and sewers. They would come out, dressed in captured German uniforms, during the night and take cover again at dawn, bringing with them food and ammunition they had obtained. The Germans replied by sending police dogs into the sewers or pumping in water or poison gas. Resistance slowly died down as the defenders were killed, but a few managed to survive and reappeared when the Russians entered Warsaw, and a few others escaped and joined the partisans. Among the fortunate ones were a young married couple, who now live in a *kibbutz* in Galilee, and whose first-born, a boy, they named Ud—that is, 'Spark'—because he had come through the fire. The struggle of the ghetto had consequences; for the great Polish rising in Warsaw a year later drew inspiration from the hopeless Jewish fight.

Warsaw was not the only place where the Jews resisted; there were similar revolts in other ghettos, and indeed desperate attempts, doomed in advance, to break out of death camps. There were Jews in the resistance movements of most occupied countries; in the French *maquis*, for example, they accounted for from fifteen to thirty per cent. Help was sent from Palestine, highly trained guerillas being parachuted into Yugoslavia to join Tito's partisans, while others were infiltrated into Hungary to organize relief. One of these, a girl aged twenty-three, has become a legendary figure in Israel, a kind of Jewish Joan of Arc. The daughter of a cultured and well-to-do family in Hungary, Hannah Shenesh had emigrated five years earlier to Palestine, where she lived in a *kibbutz* near Caesarea. Volunteering for war service, she arrived back, after many adventures, in Hungary, where her mother still lived. Some members of the Hungarian resistance movement, on learning that she was a Jew, informed the police and she was arrested and handed over to the Gestapo. Refusing to talk under severe torture, she ended her young life in front of a firing squad.

Hannah Shenesh was a poet, and young people in Israel are fond of singing one of her songs, entitled *Ashrei-ha-gafrur* (Praised be the match that is consumed as it lights the fire). The beauty of the Hebrew text is lost in translation, but the poem praises self-sacrifice, the act of dying in order that the people shall live. It may be taken as a symbol of the events I have just related.

With Hungary we have come to one of the most dramatic chapters in the history of the Jews under the Nazis.

Slowly and laboriously the wheel of fate began to turn as, little by little, the might of Germany was crushed. Early in 1944 the Red Army crossed the old frontier of Poland and on D-Day the Allied armies landed in Normandy. The German High Command knew that the war was lost and the puppet leaders began to share their opinion. One of these was Admiral Horthy, the dictator of Hungary, who had readily handed over 150,000 Transylvanian Jews for extermination. Hungary's own Jews, numbering between 500,000 and 600,000, however, he had declined to surrender and such obstinacy had to be punished. Accordingly, in March 1944 German troops marched into Budapest, where they set aside the Horthy régime and placed the Nazi Arrow Cross in its place. Eichmann and his associates of

Bureau IVA, 4b duly turned up in the wake of the German divisions, and two months later 300,000 Hungarian Jews had been consigned to Auschwitz.

Then suddenly the page of history turned. The war entered its final stages, with intriguing and secret peace feelers by leading Nazis intent on saving their own skins. One of these was Himmler himself. Unknown to Hitler and against his express orders, this once obedient servant slowed down the operations of the death factories and in time stopped them altogether. He also made secret approaches to Jewish organizations, and, early in 1945, had several interviews with Count Folke Bernadotte of Sweden. The result was the 'white bus' relief service to German concentration camps and an instruction to Eichmann in Budapest to arrange for the barter of those Hungarians who were still alive.

At once Eichmann made contact with two prominent Zionists, Dr Reszoe Kastner and Joel Brandt, cynically introducing himself as 'the bloodhound' (his own words) who had exterminated the European Jews. To the amazed Brandt he said that he was prepared to barter 100,000 Hungarian Jews for 10,000 lorries, 1000 tons of coffee, and 1000 tons of soap: *'Ware für Blut, Blut für Ware'* ('Goods for blood, blood for goods'), as he put it. But they would have to hurry.

'Ich mache Sie darauf aufmerksam, dass ich Ihnen Ihre Juden nich auf Eis legen kann' ('I warn you that I can't keep your Jews on ice').

Brandt lost no time but flew to Istanbul, leaving his family and Kastner behind as hostages. In Istanbul he transmitted the offer to the Jewish Agency, and then proceeded to Cairo to discuss the matter with the British authorities there.

The reception which Brandt got was not the one he had expected, for, believing him to be a Nazi agent, the British arrested him. When eventually he managed to obtain an interview with Lord Moyne, the British Minister in the Middle East, the latter exclaimed:

'A hundred thousand Jews! What am I to do with them? Where am I to put them?'

Whereupon Brandt replied:

'If there is no room for us anywhere, then our only alternative is the gas chambers.'

Not long after this, Lord Moyne was shot by Jewish terrorists.

The Allies, placing strategic considerations above those of humanity, were against 'trafficking with the enemy', and to supply him with lorries would have amounted to that. As an earnest of good intentions, Eichmann allowed Kastner to select a token group of 1685 Hungarian Jews for release to Switzerland at 200 dollars a head. Included in this number were 388 from Kastner's hometown, together with members of his family. In Israel, ten years later, bitter charges of saving his relatives and friends and leaving others to die were made against him, and at the trial the judge said that he had sold his soul to the Devil. A few months later he was murdered in Jerusalem.

In spite of everything, the negotiations saved many lives. But as time passed the case got increasingly urgent, and in the end Eichmann removed the last 200,000 to Bavaria. Those still surviving in Budapest were liberated by the Russians.

The curtain went up on the last act of Hitler's *Twilight of the Gods*. The Führer shot himself in the ruins of Berlin as his Third Reich crumbled; the Nazi millennium had endured for only twelve years. The Allies in the west and the Red Army in the east advanced relentlessly, finding, in concentration camps and wayside ditches, the starving remains of European Jewry after the 'final solution'. An Anglo-American committee of 1946, appointed to study the Palestine problem, arrived at the result that 87,000 Jews had survived in Greater Germany.

The butchers there had now suddenly become the hunted; but the four principal criminals of the anti-Jewish campaigns succeeded in cheating the gallows. Himmler took a lethal pill when a British patrol captured him and established his identity. Hitler also defeated justice, and Heydrich had already been dead for three years at the time of the capitulation. The fourth, Adolf Eichmann, disappeared. No one believed that he was man enough to commit suicide; his wife in Germany, whom he had neglected during the war for a fashionable mistress, held her tongue. Members of the Allied security services and the Jewish intelligence service sought him all over the world and new legends grew up around his name. One even said that he had gone to Palestine, disguised as a Jew; another, that he had recruited former German soldiers in Egypt for service against Israel in the war of 1948. At the end of 1959 it was rumoured that he had been seen in Kuwait. Whatever the facts of the matter may be, one thing is certain: some day he, too, will be rounded up. . . .[1]

Not far from Jerusalem, along a narrow road running through the mountains of Judaea, a large new building has been erected during the last few years. The contrast between its functionalistic architecture and the desolate country which surrounds it is striking. The building is Yad-Washem: a strange name taken from Isaiah which, literally translated, means 'Hand and Name', but which signifies 'A lasting memorial'. 'A name' is what remains after a man is dead; and 'hand' alludes to the ancient practice of carving a memorial in the form of a hand. Yad-Washem is the headquarters of an institution that is investigating the Jewish catastrophe under Hitlerism. Everything connected with it—documents, pictures, relics of concentration camps, accounts of survivors—is being collected in huge archives, and a staff of research workers is preparing and publishing books about it. The information given in this chapter has all been checked at Yad-Washem and is authentic.

It is difficult to arrive at an exact assessment of the number of victims. It has been estimated that the number of Jews before the war totalled 17,000,000; and in 1945 only 11,000,000 remained. In other words, 6,000,000 Jews died. Later estimates, however, suggest that this figure may be excessive, and that a more likely one is 5,000,000. Even so, it is an appalling number. In fact, Hitler went far towards achieving his aim of exterminating the Jews within his reach,

[1] The prediction turned out to be true. While this book was in production, Eichmann was kidnapped by members of the Israeli security service and taken to Israel, where his trial has since taken place.

and he maintained his hatred of them till the end. The day before he took his life in Berlin he dictated to his secretary his last will and testament, the final words of which are:

'Above all, I order the nation's leaders to carry out the racial laws down to the last detail, and to combat world Jewry which is poisoning the nations.'

The Jews were at the mercy of such hatred and the power which backed it, and moreover they stood alone. We have seen what sort of reception Brandt got in Cairo. The British authorities in Palestine, with unfailing regularity, turned back the ships carrying refugees which slipped out of Black Sea ports at incredible risk and succeeded in reaching Haifa. It is a sad fact that the Allies refused to bomb the death factories, for all the urgent appeals to them to do so. A few raids could have meant considerable delay in their activities. There were, of course, generous individuals who endeavoured to bring relief, hopeless as that seemed; but on the whole Allied action was 'too little and too late'. Henry Morgentau, President Roosevelt's Secretary to the Treasury, was provoked into the bitter comment:

'The satanic combination of British chill and diplomatic double-talk, cold and correct, and adding up to a sentence of death.'

One is reminded of Goebbels's sarcastic remarks about nations who refuse to have geniuses.

Nevertheless, there were rays of humanity which shone in the darkness and the solitude. As at Sodom, there must have been fifty men that were righteous. Their work cannot be recorded, for it was done in the deepest secrecy. But after the German collapse a few thousand Jews came forward. Brave friends and neighbours had sheltered them and enabled them to survive.

In general, however, the Germans were submissive. Though

after the war they cried a unanimous '*Ignoravimus*' ('We did not know'), others have difficulty in believing them. Many people must have known something; must have noticed, guessed at, overheard where the Jews suddenly arrested in the night had gone. If nobody spoke aloud, there must have been whispers. Yet there was never any public opinion, not even as much as to force the Government to pay a little regard to it. The only possible explanation is that centuries of anti-Semitic propaganda must have left its mark. Even after the war, when the number of Jews in Germany is less than 30,000, there have been ominous reports of outbreaks of anti-Semitism, including the desecration of graves, the chalking up of inscriptions like *Juden raus* (Jews get out), and the painting of swastikas on synagogues. There have even been astonishing statements by high officials of the West German Federal Republic. An opinion poll in 1950 showed that thirty-eight per cent of those interviewed in West Germany had anti-Semitic tendencies.

The reactions of ordinary people outside Germany differed as between East and West. In Poland they were either indifferent or they gloated over the misery of the Jews; there were some in Warsaw who applauded the pillar of fire which they saw rising from the ghetto. The behaviour of the Hungarian partisans in handing over Hannah Shenesh has already been mentioned. In Western Europe the prevailing sentiment was pity, and it did not always stop there. When the deportations began in Holland there was a general strike. The Danes helped their Jewish fellow-citizens to escape in 1943. But lest there should be any self-satisfaction, it should be added that some Jews who returned after the liberation, to both these countries, met with opposition and ill-feeling from those who had taken over their businesses.

The record of the Christian Churches is a separate story. They were the only authorities which dared to some extent to defy Hitler, and whose influence during the holocaust grew rather than it diminished. Yet their reaction to the Jewish catastrophe was not unequivocal, and there was much that is to be deplored. When the various Churches come to write their histories of this evil time they will happily be able to record many cases of courage and self-sacrifice; but they will have plenty of cause to repent and confess—especially their sins of omission.

First, the Roman Catholic Church, to which three-fourths of the population of Europe west of the old Russian frontier belonged. The official Jewish policy of the Church of Rome was formulated by Thomas Aquinas, and it presents a dual aspect. The Jews, though they were not to be exterminated, were to be humbled for their sins and obduracy. The enforced wearing of the star of David, the ghetto, the murder of Jews—none of these is new. Hitler did not invent them. They lay ready to hand, and they derive from one source—the Roman Catholic Church. The badge was introduced by the Lateran Council of 1215; Pope Paul the Fourth established the ghetto in 1555; by that time the Spanish Inquisition was in full spate. For centuries there was a prayer, said in Roman Catholic churches on Good Friday, which ran *'Oremus pro perfidis Judaeis'* ('Let us pray for the perfidious Jew'). The ugly word *'perfidis'* has only recently been removed by the present Pope, John the 23rd.

The good will shown to the Jews in their plight by Pius the Twelfth is not in doubt. He displayed it when he opened the Vatican gates and hid many of them, and also when he melted down sacred vessels in order to ransom them. Yet the solemn protest against the monstrous genocide, which all the world had expected from the Pope, never came; not even when the Germans deported 10,000 Roman Jews. This was the occasion when the German Ambassador to the Holy See, Baron Ernst von Weizsäcker, reported with satisfaction to the Foreign Ministry in Berlin:

'Though pressed from all sides, the Pope refused to be pushed into any form of censure on the deportation of the Jews from Rome. . . .'

The same varying image is displayed by the Protestant Churches. From Luther to Stöcker, the Court chaplain in Berlin, runs a direct line of Jewish hatred. Had they known the

Second World War, they would have seen the fruits of their words. Nevertheless, there were bishops both in Germany and in the occupied countries who dared to speak out. On the first Sunday after the German raids a solemn protest was read from every Danish pulpit.

The Jews have learnt a costly lesson. The vision of smoking chimneys over crematoria where their fellows went by the million to an anonymous and merciless death has seemed like a nightmare to them. And who is to say that this has been the last time, and that Germany is the only country where such things could happen? In the crucible of horror a new Jew is being created, as was foreshadowed by the figure of Theodor Herzl.

Israel now knows that the real *Endlösung der jüdischen Frage* is not to be looked for in Oriental resignation and passivity. The Jewish people have taken their destiny into their own hands. Here, also, the words of the Psalm have come true:

'They that sow in tears shall reap in joy.'

III

THE KREMLIN

꧂

THE night silence was broken with such suddenness that events were in full swing before anyone was properly awake. Rifle butts hammered on an ill-fitting door, the lock was forced, and the door flew open with a jerk.

'Out you get!'

At the bark of command the occupants of the house were at last aroused. There was a yelp from the dog as it was kicked by a soldier's boot. Sleepy eyes peering from under the blankets in the light of a pocket torch saw police constables brandishing knouts.

'You are to leave at once. Get out. Anybody found still here at dawn will be strung up on the nearest door post.'

Wearing their scanty clothing they staggered out into the freezing winter night. The same scene was repeated all over the Jewish quarter of this small West Russian town. When a few hundred Jews had been rounded up the constables pushed them off along the road—children, old people, able-bodied men and women carrying invalids on their backs—all on foot, because this time there were no trucks. The constables belaboured them with their knouts when they did not go fast enough.

The same took place in every town where there were Jews—in Courland, Lithuania, Poland. If the town was served by a railway station the victims were fortunate and were crowded into cattle trucks and driven off, with the doors barred, for several days at a stretch.

It was the first winter of the First World War and the Russian army was in full retreat before Hindenburg. Loyal to their Czarist master, the Russian generals were convinced that the Jews would turn traitors. Were they not already known to have aided the enemy, by sending him their gold tied to the wings of swans, and by transmitting intelligence to spies? Forgotten, it seems, was the fact that half a million Jews were serving in the Russian army, and that many had already been decorated for gallantry. It has been estimated that 100,000 people died during the mass deportations of that Russian winter.

The tide of war engulfed those countries in which three-fourths of the world's Jews were then living—Poland, Western Russia, Lithuania, and Galicia—as the Russian, Austrian, and German armies advanced and retreated in turns. As the tide receded it left behind the ruins of towns and villages and of many human lives.

Yet the war itself was only the beginning of the misery. In 1917 the Czarist régime was swept aside; in November of the same year the revolutionary Government of Kerensky was itself overthrown by the Bolsheviks under Lenin.

In the period that followed a small band of Jews wielded greater power than any had ever done before, among them Trotsky, Sverdelev, Zinoviev, Litvinov, Radek, Yoffe, and Kaganovich, to name only some of the more prominent among them. There was a comparatively high proportion of leading Jewish politicians on the left wing. In this fact there is nothing remarkable, in view of the treatment which Jews suffered under Czarism. The Czar himself they hated, reserving for him their bitterest curse, 'Yemah shemo!' ('May his name be obliterated!'). But none of these revolutionary leaders had preserved the ties with their Jewish past; they were all fully assimilated.

What is more, they had no mass following among other Jews. In spite of their degradation under Czarism, it is a fact that the majority of Russian Jews did not support Bolshevism. Most of them belonged to the Liberal Party, and the Jewish Socialist Bund was associated with the moderate Mensheviks. It was a Jewess, Dora Kaplan, who made the attempt on Lenin's life.

After the war and revolution came civil war. First Petlura in the Ukraine clashed with Trotsky's new Red Army; then Denikin's White Army turned on both Trotsky and Petlura. On one thing, however, Petlura and Denikin were agreed, and that was that the Jews were identical with the Godless régime in the Kremlin, that they were synonymous with anti-Christ and had to be eliminated. Scenes of incredible sadism were the result: the Jewish quarters were cleared, there was wholesale looting by soldiers and partisans, many Jews died; the Ukraine especially witnessed a reign of terror. To avert the same fate as the Jews, Christians took to painting crosses on their doors. The worst of the generals was Petlura, whose conduct recalled that of the hetman Bogdan Chmielnicki, who had brought fire and sword to the Ukraine in 1648. Petlura came to a sudden end in 1926, when a young man, by name Shlomo Schwarzbart, who had witnessed the murder of his father by guerillas, shot him in a Paris restaurant. The assassin was acquitted by a French court.

By 1920 the Red Army had prevailed, and Lenin and his men embarked on the task of restoring order out of chaos. From Czarism they had inherited the difficult problem of regulating relations with the Jews, of whom 2,500,000 remained after the post-war reduction of territory. What their fate has been, in general, is not fully known, but it is possible to glean something from the scraps of information which from time to time have come out of Russia, and it is a clear enough picture that we get. As background there is the classical Communist view of the Jewish question.

It is a slick argument to assert that Communism is a Jewish invention. It is true that Karl Marx was a Jew, but by birth only, not ideologically. Throughout his life he was hostile to Jewry and despised what he called 'this figment of a people'. As Marx saw it, the stock exchange and the Jews were one.

We can pass to Lenin, the official apostle of modern Communism, who soon made up his mind about the Jews. At the time of the split between Bolsheviks and Mensheviks in 1903 the Jews had no place in the programme Lenin then submitted. It is possible to detect a dualism in Lenin's thinking. Anti-Semitism, as a prime political weapon of the Czarist régime, demonstrated in the pogroms, was obviously to be condemned. The true Communist was a champion of Jewish emancipation, though at the same time he had certain reservations. The principle of national self-determination did not apply to the Jews, because they were not a nation as Lenin understood it: they did not occupy a common territory, they had no common language, and there was no settled Jewish peasantry. Jewry was a relic of the Middle Ages, artificially maintained by pressure and persecution but eventually doomed to extinction. Lenin's solution of the Jewish problem was assimilation.

In 1913, exactly ten years after the declaration of Bolshevik policy, Lenin allowed his obedient disciple Joseph Djugashvili to elaborate his theses. Writing under his party name of Joseph Stalin, the latter called the Jews 'a paper nation, still without evidence of its existence'. Stalin was always bitterly anti-Semitic. Since, as already mentioned, the majority of Jews were not Bolsheviks, at the most were Mensheviks, he once said, with one of his grim jokes, 'perhaps we ought to arrange a pogrom in the party'.

Even in its early days, when it consisted wholly of despised or unknown sectarians, the party was actively engaged in formulating its anti-Jewish programme. The policy of Lenin and Stalin was aimed at eliminating the Jewish characteristics by complete assimilation. It is still the policy of the Communist rulers today. As in other aspects of Russian policy, there have been changes in the party line from time to time; concessions and repressions have alternated; double-talk has been common. But always behind the somersaults one clear policy has been discernible. The brief periods of indulgence have been no more than tactics and window-dressing. As soon as it suited their book the Kremlin reversed their policy, reverting to the long-term one which they have never abandoned. That is aimed at the elimination of Jewry, first in Russia and later in the world at large.

In spite of assimilation and the horrors of war, the Russian Jews remained a live and vigorous community, far removed from the character of pariahs that was sometimes given to them by Communist propaganda. Living in the cities of Western Europe, but more particularly in many small towns (called in Yiddish *shtetl*, from the German *Städtlein*), they had evolved a Jewish culture in synagogues, schools, Talmud academies, and books and newspapers, both Yiddish and Hebrew, and they clung to it through every kind of persecution over the centuries. Russian Jewry is quite distinctive, and it has vitality and powers of resistance far exceeding those of any other of Russia's numerous national minorities.

The Kerensky Government had suddenly emancipated them. Every restriction was at once abolished and they were able to look forward hopefully to the future. It was a short-lived happiness which lasted for eight months, from March 1917 until November. The period of Soviet rule which then began has now lasted for some forty-five years.

The Bolsheviks at first were lenient. The segregation of Czarist days was abolished and Jews were permitted to live wherever they liked. Anti-Semitism was punishable by death. As part of a large-scale educational campaign, loyal Communists were urged in posters to combat 'ignorance, alcoholism, and anti-Semitism'. Lenin was shrewd; the minorities obviously could not be eliminated at a single stroke, and so for a time they were handled carefully.

Like the rest, the Jews were given certain cultural rights, though they did not include the use of the Hebrew language; being associated with religion and Zionism, that was taboo. Schools (*hederim*) and colleges (*yeshivot*) where it had been kept alive were quite simply forbidden. At the same time, the colloquial Yiddish was unrestricted. State-run Yiddish schools appeared in the Ukraine and White Russia, Yiddish was made a judicial language in districts with many Jewish inhabitants, Yiddish newspapers and books circulated freely, local authorities supported Yiddish theatres. In the Soviet Union at one time there were no fewer than sixteen State-run Yiddish theatres, including the celebrated Moscow theatre where the Jewish actor Shlomo Mikhoels was the director.

At the same time there were clear-eyed Jews whose reaction to this trend was mixed. While happy to see an end to restrictions, they could not rid themselves of a fear that there was a trap in it. This was not the first time in Russian history that the government had provided State aid for Jewish culture. Nearly a hundred years earlier, Czar Nicholas the First had established schools for Jews, but they had not used them, fearing that their purpose was to undermine Jewry. In this case, too, they suspected treachery. It would not be sudden, but the plans would be laid gradually. Still, it was the only way whereby children could obtain an education, and so most parents sent them to the schools.

While the Kremlin gave with one hand it took away with the other; for the Jews were deprived of their system of self-government. The network of Jewish communities known as *kehillot*, which had regulated Jewish affairs for centuries, was suddenly banned. Instead, Jewish matters were placed under a special section of the Communist Party, called the *Yevsektsia*. Its officials proved to be abysmally ignorant of Jewish life and saw it as their prime object to instruct Jews in Communist ideology.

Feverishly, the government embarked upon the economic and social revolution that was to transform the old Russia into the world's first Communist State. It went quickly, and indeed it went too quickly. The haste was soon reflected in economic crises and collapses, which involved the people in further heavy sacrifices and sufferings; millions died in prolonged periods of starvation. The subsequent NEP period and the Five Year Plans brought more upheavals for the masses. In all this the Jews shared the experience of other Russians. Tens of thousands of the inhabitants of the old *shtetl* were industrialized; many former tailors, small traders, pedlars, and scrap-dealers are now factory workers. Many Jews, being generally of a higher cultural standard than the average Russian, found their way to high positions in the administration.

Russia is an ancient agricultural country. But war, revolution, and their aftermath disorganized peasant life; in the 1920s great areas lay waste, their inhabitants having died or fled. In order to provide bread, the Government was forced to intervene. Thus a new chapter was written in Jewish history as the Soviet authorities strove to change many of them into modern farmers. In the Ukraine and the Crimea, two of the areas that had suffered most, large collective farms, called *kolkhoz*, were established for Jews. The experiment was watched with excitement by observers abroad, and Jewish relief organizations collected funds to finance it. The experiment was short-lived. As the Stalinist purges gained headway in the 1930s, most of the Jews were removed from the collectives and were replaced by orthodox Communists.

More remarkable still is the history of Birobijan, a province of Eastern Siberia, separated from Manchuria by the Amur river. Russia here had need of a buffer against Japanese expansion and Chinese colonization in what was a sparsely populated area. Birobijan is rich in timber and mineral resources, but its climate is unsuitable for Europeans, and so it was difficult to get Russians to settle there. Other means had to be found.

Suddenly, in 1934, the Kremlin proclaimed the establishment of the self-governing Jewish province of Birobijan. It was typical of the way the Soviet authorities operated. This was an opportunistic move intended to kill two birds with one stone. In the first place, the Jews would surely be tempted by this promising offer of self-government; in the second, the world would be offered a plausible alternative to Zionism. It could be argued that the Soviet Government was giving to the Jews the State they so eagerly wanted. Moreover, it could be expected that financial assistance would be sent from abroad, and the Soviet can always use dollars.

The propaganda value of Birobijan was exploited, for years, to the utmost, the life of the Jewish settlers there being presented in the most glowing colours. The reality was altogether different. The climate was so severe that many Jews soon gave up, and disappeared. The latest information about the province dates from 1959 when the twenty-fifth anniversary was celebrated. The population then was 163,000, of whom only 34,000 were Jews.

Neither of the two rivers which gave the province of Birobijan its name is any sort of Jordan, and never will be.

The first week of November 1917 marked a turning-point in Jewish history. By a strange coincidence, two events that were to have a profound effect on Jewish destinies took place in that week. On November 2, 1917, the British Government made the Balfour Declaration which opened the doors of Palestine to Jewish settlement; and five days later, on November 7, Lenin gained control in Russia. It was like the start of a race between two forces; and it is symbolical of the conflict between Zionism and Communism. From that week the rivalry has proceeded, in a steadily rising climax, from one crisis to another. Beginning as tension between two opposed ideologies, it ended by becoming a world problem of the first order. Sooner or later it was obvious that there would be a collision; for the two forces are as opposite as fire and water. The Soviet régime sees the only solution of the Jewish problem in assimilation; the Jews are to cease to be Jews and become Russians. Zionism seeks the opposite; its aim is to bring the homeless Jews of the Dispersal together and weld them into a nationally conscious people in the land of their forefathers.

The first skirmishes began in 1917, when the Communists accused the Zionists of being 'a tool of British Imperialism and Western colonization'. Behind the veiled threat the Soviet authorities were able to exert pressure. They had barely consolidated their rule when the Zionist organization in the Ukraine was dissolved, and from then on things moved quickly. The Zionists of Russia have experienced more than one night of terror, with the secret police hammering on their doors. Thousands disappeared into penal camps up and down the vast country, in places ranging from the Solovetski Islands in the White Sea to Siberia, places where it is said that 'winter lasts for twelve months, and the rest of the year is summer'. In Soviet Russia Zionism is a crime, the very name being among

the worst of insults. As recently as October 1956 an enraged
Khrushchev hurled it at the head of Gomulka during a violent
scene in the Warsaw *politbureau*.

Zionism in Russia is far older than the name itself. Theodor
Herzl was still unconverted when Leo Pinsker, an Odessa
doctor, put new life into his persecuted fellow-Jews by pointing
to the old land. The Lovers of Zion (*Hoveve Zion*), a pioneer
group in Palestine under Turkish rule, came from Russia, as
did many of those who founded the State of Israel, chief among
them Chaim Weizmann, its first President.

But under the Soviets the Zionist movement has had to go
under ground; it is now an illegal movement, operating from
secret cells. An idea is one thing, and its realization another;
and the Russian Zionists have had to be content with the idea.
The great ambition of getting out of Russia and reaching the
promised land is a dream which only one in a million can ever
hope to realize. At the same time, the existence of the idea and
the work of teaching it to others gives inspiration, as well as
self-respect. The Resistance in German-occupied countries
endured many bitter disappointments, but all was well in the
end, though the days became months and the months years.
Russian Zionism has now experienced a winter that has lasted
half a century. It provides many examples of inspiring courage,
endurance, and humorous relief, of which the following are
a few.

It was an October day in 1924 and the congregations were leaving
the synagogues of Odessa after celebrating the joyful feast of
Simhat-Tora. Outside each of the synagogues groups of young
people stood singing the *Hatikvah*, now the national anthem of
Israel and even then a rallying song of Zionism. Not long after
this, the education authorities in the Ukraine received tens of
thousands of anonymous letters, all in children's handwriting,
asking for the reintroduction of Hebrew as a school subject.
There could be little doubt that the demonstration had been
organized by Zionists, but the police never traced them. These
may be small things, but they are symptomatic of the fighting
spirit which inspires them.

More important were the efforts which Zionists and the Komsomol, the Communist youth organization, exerted in order to infiltrate into each other's ranks. The Komsomol were the losers. They over-credulously accepted 'repentant' Zionists, who thus gained an opportunity to undermine their work. The Zionists, being more used to this sort of struggle, put their candidates to so severe a test that would-be informers were excluded along with others who could not, if necessary, have withstood police investigation.

Thousands of Zionists have been deported, over the years, to remote parts of the Soviet Union. It is known that many of them never lost heart, and indeed a few succeeded in escaping, through Iran or Afghanistan, to Palestine. Even those less fortunate achieved other results. In the 1920s the post office censorship in these isolated parts remained ignorant of the illegal activities of the Zionists, and consequently letters to and from Palestine were transmitted. As a result, the deportees knew more about current events in the developing centre of Jewry than people living at liberty in other parts of Russia. Aware, moreover, that their letters home were rarely forwarded, they began writing via Palestine, from where their correspondence was relayed. The Jews in Palestine became skilled in the writing of clandestine letters, and at concealing their meaning between the lines.

Even in Russia the Zionists were not wholly friendless. One of their sympathizers was the world-famous writer Maxim Gorky, together with his first wife, Yekaterina Pavlovna Peshkova, who succeeded in obtaining exit visas for some and reduction of sentences for others, and who sent gift parcels to prisons.

Russian policies have been world-wide, and this also holds good of their attitude to Zionism. In the 1920s and 1930s the Kremlin openly and secretly supported the Arab rulers in Palestine against the British and the Jewish settlers. This policy has been continued down to the present day, and since September 1955 has found dangerous manifestation in military and political aid to the Arab countries. In this matter the

Soviet Union is playing a dangerous game, using its anti-Zionism as a pawn in the Cold War. In the Middle East it employs it as a welcome instrument with which to attack British oil and strategic interests. At the same time, it has not prevented the Kremlin from zigzagging. In 1947 came one of those reversals of tactics that are so characteristic of Russian policy.

The General Assembly of the United Nations was discussing the Palestine problem, which once again had reached a deadlock. Suddenly and dramatically, the Russian delegate announced his support for the division of Palestine into an Arab and a Jewish part, and of course the satellites followed suit. With this the issue was decided, the resolution getting the required two-thirds majority. With this backing, David Ben-Gurion a few months later proclaimed the State of Israel, and he had scarcely done so when Russia accorded the new nation its recognition. World statesmen were surprised and talked of a radical change in Russian policy to the Jews, but those who were best informed did not share this naïve and unrealistic view.

In fact, the matter was clear: Russia had seen an opportunity to force the British out of one of their major bastions, and to this end she cynically supported, in Zionism, what she had before bitterly opposed. Russia is ready at all times to pay what it costs to achieve an objective, even if it means denying her past; she merely sacrifices a lesser advantage to win a greater one. Then as soon as the point is gained, she reverts to her old position. That was what happened in this case. Since 1952 Russia has consistently voted against Israel in the United Nations, and used her veto against her on all possible occasions.

It may seem strange that the rulers of this giant country should get so nervous at the least sign of Zionism, a few men among millions, or be upset by the tiny country of Israel; but in the Kremlin they weigh the little things, and they know that Israel is firmly pro-Western and will always cherish the ideals of the free world. They feel that it is intolerable that even so small a group as the Zionists in Russia should feel attachment for a foreign State, especially when it is one that cannot be brought under control. For such pretensions there can only be the full penalty of State prohibition.

After so many years of repression it may seem surprising that Zionism should ever have survived, but one need only ask the Kremlin, which has paid it the compliment of holding it up as the root of all evil. The intellectuals who fell victim to Stalin's purges were accused of it, as were the victims of the Slansky trial in Prague in 1952, in which eleven of the fourteen accused were Jews.

It need hardly be said that the movement which once flourished has been broken up; but given favourable conditions it may quickly be reunited and revived. That there are Russian Jews who listen in to the Israeli radio is shown by incidents like the one told by an official of the Israeli Embassy in Moscow. He was walking one day in the street when an unknown stranger whispered, as he passed:

'It was seventy-seven degrees in Tel Aviv at eight this morning.'

'My time is eternal; but yours was up before it began.'

The bold words were spoken by a rabbi to his judge. He had been brought before one of those public circuses which the League of Militant Atheists likes to arrange in order to make fun of religion. The target in this case was Judaism and the accused was the religious school (*heder*); the rabbi had been summoned in its defence. Time was running short, and the judge could allow him only five minutes for the defence; as he spoke, he looked at his watch. At the end of the five minutes he struck the table with his hammer, and cried:

'Your time's up.' And then came the rabbi's swift reply:

'My time is eternal. Yours was up before it began.'

His words may be taken as a motto for the struggle between Communism and religion in Soviet Russia.

'Religion is opium for the people.' This oft-quoted thesis of Karl Marx is the watchword under which the Communists wage war on the religious front. Officially there is religious liberty in Russia, but at the same time the bias is clearly in favour of atheism. The question is formulated in the Soviet Constitution in the words 'There is freedom for religious confession and anti-religious propaganda.' In other words, religious people may exist but must be silent; only atheists may actively propagate their ideas. The Godless are organized in the League of Militant Atheists just mentioned; and in their fanaticism they resemble the Orthodox Church of Czarist times. It would be fair to call them religious atheists.

These militant atheists started operations in the 1920s, and they are still very active. Their campaigns in areas of Jewish settlement have not merely been popular in form, they have sometimes been downright vulgar. Neither church nor synagogue could feel safe from their interference. There have been occasions when noisy crowds have burst in to the service, perhaps dragging a pig behind them, as they shouted in chorus:

'For God is a pig, the mightiest of all pigs. Amen.'

The devout were even molested in their homes, as the children would be encouraged by their teachers to interrupt their praying by singing Communist songs. The newspapers waged daily propaganda either by caricaturing religion or by branding it as a reactionary force responsible for attacks on education and the Communist State. Young Jews were indoctrinated against it in study groups which they were forced to attend, and in which the Bible was misrepresented, the patriarchs, kings, and prophets, who had been honoured names in the home, being represented as reactionary or ignorant. Jacob would be called a trickster; Joseph the son of Jacob, a kulak, who hoarded the corn of Egypt and even sold it abroad, leaving the Egyptian masses to starve; Moses, far from being a liberator, was shown as a demagogue, who had lured the Hebrews into the wilderness and thereby prevented them from rising in revolt against the tyranny of Pharaoh. The religious schools were not alone in being ridiculed; so too, were the *Kol Nidre* ritual of the Day of Atonement, and the *seder* of the eve of the Passover. Judge, prosecutor, defence counsel, witnesses—the whole setting of the court was a mockery. Occasionally, however, a brave man like the rabbi quoted would speak words that would bring a moment's silence to the court and would be remembered by everyone there that day. The story of that rabbi has a sequel.

It goes without saying that his courage was punished; the penalty was two years' imprisonment. In the prison, however, he found enough fellow-Jews to form a *minyan*, the quorum of ten men that is required for a service, and on the eve of the Day of Atonement they held their service. Their singing woke the warders, and they feared the consequences; but to their astonishment these men were deeply moved, and crossed themselves. One even asked to be confessed.

Anti-religious propaganda is of course supported by the Government in its entirety. Though the authorities never take part officially, the campaigns reflect official policy. This is true of all religion, not only of Judaism; but in the case of the Jews their religion is of special importance, since if they are to be assimilated it is essential to strike at the roots of their religion. If that goes, then the Jew ceases to be a Jew in any real sense. This the Kremlin knows, aiming its blows, therefore, where they will have most effect. The Soviet attitude to religion can be studied nowhere better than in the case of Judaism.

An endless succession of laws and decrees has stripped the Russian Jews of almost all that in the past gave colour and distinction to their lives. Synagogues, schools, hospitals, and charitable institutions have been closed and their property confiscated, the buildings being now used as club rooms, libraries, cinemas, and warehouses. Their cemeteries have been laid out as public parks. If one of the few remaining synagogues needs repair, it is extremely difficult to obtain a licence. Those that do remain are far from adequate for their congregations.

Even the services are hampered. It may be a small point, but the Feast of the Tabernacle now has to be celebrated without the traditional lemons, palms, myrtles, and willow twigs. A bigger interference is the prohibition of *kosher* or ritual slaughter, which renders it impossible to observe the Law with regard to the food that a Jew may eat. The new calendar makes it extremely difficult to keep the Sabbath and celebrate the great festivals. Then there are innumerable pinpricks, including the popular one of accusing the rabbis of tax evasion. In the anti-religious museum in Moscow there is a special section devoted to demonstrating the superstition and archaism of Judaism. The other religious communities are led by national organizations and Judaism alone has no central body, but is split and incohesive. Moslems may go on pilgrimage to Mecca, but Jews may not go to Palestine.

Many more repressive measures could be enumerated, but those already mentioned are sufficient to illustrate the chill atmosphere which has surrounded religion since 1917. Most of the customs previously associated with Jewish life have fallen into disuse. Russian Jewry, once so flourishing, is no longer in the mainstream of creative culture but has been driven into a stagnant backwater. Delegations who have visited Russia in order to study the religious lives of the Jews have returned home with depressing reports, saying that the congregations in synagogues consist of old people, and that the young have little knowledge of the religion of their forefathers and still less interest in it. It is no wonder, when the authorities restrict religious activities and prohibit religious teaching. The much-praised religious freedom of Russia seems, indeed, to be limited to allowing people to attend service and to observe the traditional funeral rites.

Yet the fact remains that these foreign visitors see only the surface. Below it, hidden from the prying eyes of the police, Judaism still lives on in its ancient vigour. Following Zionism, it too went under ground. Like the *marran* under the Spanish Inquisition, many Russian Jews live a double life, outwardly resembling their neighbours but being practising Jews in the privacy of their homes, cherishing their traditions as far as they are able and teaching their children to do the same. It follows that very little can be told about this secret life; but we do know that there is a religious underground movement with a secret network of schools which teach Hebrew, the Bible, and the Talmud.

The darkness is illumined by small flashes of light. In the 1930s the job of night watchman was popular with rabbis. They earned their living at the work, and in the dead of night their disciples would come to them and get instruction in the sacred books. There is a joke which dates from that time.

'One day, by God's will, all will change and the good old times will return. If when that happens a man lays claim to teach the *Torah* and practise as a rabbi, say to him: "Show me first your night watchman's certificate."'

There have been some brave men among the Russian rabbis, and their message is eternal and unconquerable. The rabbi who refused an opportunity to emigrate to the United States in order to stay with his people knew that. It was about the same time that he met a colleague who was in the throes of despair, feeling that everything was in vain. 'Can a dead man be brought to life by an injection?' the colleague asked. His answer was:

'A body which can still feel pain is not dead. Your fear proves that Judaism is alive.'

Another exchange took place a few years later, in a synagogue. A well-known Israeli who was attending a service there saw a fifteen-year-old boy come in. It was the anniversary of his father's death, and tradition required that he should say the *Kaddish*, or prayer for the dead.

'Do you understand Hebrew?' the man asked.

'No, I haven't learnt it.'

'Yiddish, perhaps?'

'No, nor that either.'

'Well, you must know something about the Jewish faith?'

'Where would I hear that?'

'Why are you here, when you know neither Hebrew nor your own religion?' was the astonished question. The boy answered simply:

'Because I am a Jew.'

'I don't understand. Where did you learn that from?'
The boy pointed to his left side, and said:
'*Tut.*' *Tut* is the Russian for 'here'.
We can doubtless regard his reply as symbolical of the attitude of Jewish youth in Russia to the faith of their fathers.

The year 1930 marks a decisive point in the history of the Russian Jews. This was the time when Trotsky was deposed and Stalin gained control. In 1930 Stalin opened his campaign against the Jews. Before then the Kremlin had calculated on the effects of alternate repression and relaxation to break down their resistance, but now its patience was exhausted. In the purges of the 1930s, when Stalin liquidated the opposition, one of the principal instruments which he used was anti-Semitism. Trotsky was a Jew, as were Zinoviev, Kamenev, and Radek, three of the executed inner council; and anti-Semitic sentiments were played upon by the prosecutor at the trial. From then on the repressions were intensified. The *Yevsektsia* were abolished, as also were Yiddish schools and the Jewish *kolkhoz*. The purge bit deep into the ranks of the Jews. At the time, the Jewish proportion of the population was two per cent; but ten per cent of those sentenced to death were Jews. The Zionist and illegal religious groups were almost wiped out.

If the 1930s were bad, the 1940s were even worse. War came to Russia on June 22, 1941. The massacre of Jews by the ss in Russia has already been described. But even behind the front there were menacing shadows, Stalin realized that the Jews could be used in the service of Russian propaganda; they had millions of fellows in the United States. Accordingly, he ordered a Jewish Anti-Fascist League to be set up in Moscow with Shlomo Mikhoels, the popular actor, as its president, and with well-known Jews as prominent members, among them the author Ilya Ehrenburg, officers, and rabbis. Many of these had forgotten that they had ever been Jews; they were assimilated, and had no wish to appear publicly as Jews. They had no choice. The business of the League was to furnish newspapers in the

free world with articles about the workers' fatherland, the
Jewish paradise, the land now waging an heroic war to liberate
European Jewry from Hitlerism, a war in which Russian Jews
were among the bravest.

The rosy picture of Russian Jewry intended for foreign use
was never displayed at home; no Russian newspaper ever printed
any of the articles. Even at the fronts, it was quite another
picture; for there the political commissars, the *politruk*, Stalin's
spies and lackeys, were in control. It was their task to ensure that
the population in German occupation, or in liberated areas,
should support the Russian cause and aid the Red Army.
These West Russian areas are the ancient centres of anti-
Semitism; and the commissars did not scruple to exploit it, with
pitiful consequences to the Jews. Jewish guerillas, who had
perhaps escaped German persecution by the skin of their teeth,
were informed upon by partisans or mown down in ambushes.
Unbelievable as it may seem, there were occasions when the
partisans opened a second front against Jewish units, to the
detriment of the real war against the Germans. The spirit was
no better in the regular army. General Zhukov, the hero of
Stalingrad, expressed his open contempt for Jewish troops; and
General Anders, the Polish army leader, refused to have Jewish
volunteers in his units.

As the war drew to a close and the German deluge receded, it
was seen to have left a mass of jetsam behind it. The Germans
had been feared and hated in the occupied countries and none
of their ideology had made any impression on the Russians
except in the one case of anti-Semitism. On this, German
troops and Russian peasants were as one. All the old hatred of
the Jews in Russia was stimulated during the years of occupation, and it did not die down after the Germans had left. Three
years later, in 1948, the time was ripe for the most violent
persecution since the days of Plehve, the Czar's Minister of the
Interior and instigator of the pogrom at Kishinev.

The man chosen to fire the first shot was Ilya Ehrenburg.
Troubled all his life by his Jewish origin, this great writer has
found his mind a battlefield of conflicting impulses. Fleeing

from Russia in his youth, he had lived in Paris, where he had written novels with an anti-Soviet bias and been applauded by Russian *émigrés*. In the 1930s he had returned home like the prodigal son and been welcomed with the fatted calf. Ehrenburg dutifully danced to Stalin's pipe in the matter of the Jews. Having previously led his fellow-writers in extolling Jewish achievements, he now sniffed the wind and resigned from the League. He is one of the few former members who are still alive.

In January 1948 Ehrenburg came out with the article which started the persecution. Perhaps it was not very sensational; all it did was to revive the old argument that the Jews were not a nation, but it foreshadowed things to come. From that day on the Jewish intelligentsia ceased to sleep on pillows, but instead rested their heads on small travel bags, expecting nightly visits from the secret police.

The first man to be taken was Shlomo Mikhoels. He was with fellow-actors at Minsk when a telephone call came for him; and his friends never saw him alive again. He was said to have died in a traffic accident, but an inquest was not allowed, and there were clear signs that his head had been battered in a struggle. Mikhoels' funeral was attended by big demonstrations, when tens of thousands filed past his coffin. The subsequent liquidations went off more quietly, the victims being quietly picked up and never heard of again. All told, 443 writers, painters, actors, and teachers disappeared—the flower of Jewish intelligence. At the same time, the authorities exerted great efforts to inflame public opinion against the Jews. The newspapers were filled with accusations against the 'bourgeois-imperialist elements and rootless cosmopolitan types', that subverted Soviet life and infiltrated capitalist-nationalistic influences. Their target was Zionism, which they chose to regard as an international conspiracy to reintroduce capitalism into the Soviet Union and the popular-democratic republics. In the holocaust a rich literature in Yiddish was destroyed, and Yiddish publications ceased to appear. It is only in the last few years that a few Yiddish classics have again been issued in tiny editions.

Even then the Soviet Union spoke with two tongues. While the persecutions were being planned, Vishinsky was warmly supporting the Jewish cause in Palestine from the platform of the United Nations General Assembly. We have seen how the Russians supported a resolution calling for a Jewish State.

There was one incident in Moscow which must have made Stalin think. The first Israeli Ambassador to Moscow was Mrs Golda Meir, now the Foreign Minister in Jerusalem, and she announced that she would attend the service on the Day of Atonement in Moscow's biggest synagogue. On the way there her car was blocked by crowds of people, all of them Jews. Hearing that 'their own' ambassador was coming, they had turned out to welcome her. This striking demonstration of a secret Jewry just outside the Kremlin walls was not the last of its kind.

The Slansky trial in Prague showed that anti-Semitism could be used in other countries behind the Iron Curtain besides Russia, while in the months which preceded the death of Stalin in March 1953 his anti-Semitism assumed megalomanic forms. In this period nine prominent doctors, seven of whom were Jews, were arrested on the charge of conspiring to poison Stalin, together with members of the Politbureau and the General Staff. It was alleged that they were members of an international band operating through the American relief organization Joint, the agent of Imperialism. This was a new version of the hoary Protocols of the Elders of Zion, which, then as now, was the work of the Russian secret police, whose approach seems to have changed but little since the days of Czarism. Two of the doctors died in gaol, but the others were saved by Stalin's death and were subsequently released. Stalin's heirs said that a regrettable mistake had been made.

Nikita Khrushchev is a native of the Ukraine, where he was born in 1894, and where he began his career. In 1938, as first party secretary, he occupied the highest post there; during the war he was made head of the partisan army and organized guerilla war activities. They called him 'Stalin's eye'. The deep-seated anti-Semitism of the Ukraine was imprinted in

Khrushchev's mind. For proof one need only recall a remark he is fond of making:

'A second-rate Kovalsky is worth more than a first-rate Rosenblum.'

'There are too many Abramoviches here,' he sneered in Poland. (Rosenblum and Abramovich are, of course, common Jewish names.)

It is noteworthy that when he revealed the Stalinist crimes, at the celebrated Twentieth Party Congress in 1956, Khrushchev had nothing to say about the persecutions of the Jews. Sometimes silence speaks louder than words. It is true that some of the liquidated Jewish intellectuals have been 'rehabilitated'. But rehabilitation is given little publicity. The newspapers will announce that a man's books are being reprinted, and his widow will get a small gratuity.

But the living are more important than the dead, and what of them? The removal of Kaganovich in 1957 saw the Politbureau purged of the last of its Jews. His fault was not that he was a Jew, but that he had belonged to the Molotov-Malenkov group; but it is symptomatic that now few Jews, if any, occupy leading party posts or hold senior army and diplomatic rank. Again, the 1932 edition of the official Soviet encyclopedia included 160 columns about the Jews, whereas the latest edition has only eight, and four of them are about Birobijan. Furthermore, the Government-controlled radio puts out, from time to time, gross accusations about the Jews, as well as reports of mob violence resembling pogroms, in which the police do not interfere. In October 1959, during the Jewish New Year, the synagogue at Malakhova, near Moscow, was set alight.

Khrushchev knows that no detail of Soviet policy, except for its suppression of the Hungarian revolution, has been so abhorrent to the free world as the anti-Jewish campaigns. Occasionally, therefore, some slight relief is allowed; but on the whole the same general policy is followed.

From the Sinai campaign: a bombed Egyptian convoy

Egyptian troops surrendering

Israeli troops with a captured portrait of Nasser

Israeli naval flag flying over a captured Egyptian destroyer

Egyptian officers in a prison camp

On guard in the Gulf of Aqaba

For the last twenty centuries a country's Jewish policy has been a measure of its enlightenment. The conclusion of this chapter must be that Communism is an even greater menace than Hitler was.

Early in 1960 the Soviet authorities informed the United Nations' Committee on Minority Rights that there were 3,000,000 Jews in Russia. A census a few weeks later showed that there were only 2,268,000, and no explanation has been given to account for the difference. In fact, a careful survey based on information which cannot be divulged supports the larger figure. It follows that there are 3,000,000 souls that the Communists have consistently failed, during more than forty years, to assimilate. Even young people born after the revolution have resisted assimilation and still feel that they are Jews.

In October 1957 a World Youth Congress was held in Moscow and a delegation attended from Israel, accompanied by a group of singers and dancers. From Odessa the Israelis travelled to Moscow by train. They were so moved by the reception which they got that they wept when they told about it.

As their ship docked at Odessa they found thousands of Jews waiting for them on the quayside, and every station at which they stopped on the way to Moscow was crowded with people, some just silently watching, others wanting eagerly to touch the visitors, to beg a badge or other souvenir, a picture postcard or a scrap of a Hebrew newspaper. The theatre at which the Israelis appeared was packed to capacity. They were billed for the first half, and when they left at the interval the audience left with them, leaving the Yugoslavs, who followed, to play before empty seats. The following evening the Israelis were due to appear at a large theatre in the centre of Moscow, but were informed, an hour or two before the performance, that for 'technical reasons' they were being transferred to another theatre. This turned out to be a small suburban theatre, six miles from the centre, seating only two hundred people. Arriving there just before the show, the Israelis found the square in front of the theatre crowded with people. The many hundreds who had bought tickets for the other theatre had come, not to get in, for they knew there would be no room, but merely to see the Israelis as they entered and left the theatre.

Things like this demonstrate to the Kremlin that its policy has failed, and that the Jews cannot be assimilated; and as soon as Khrushchev and his associates fully understand this, they will be obliged to draw the conclusions. They will have to throw open the gates and allow the Jews to emigrate. It may be long, but the time will surely come when the Kremlin must listen to the cry: Let my people go.

In a synagogue in Jerusalem stands a rabbi's chair. It is remarkable in that it lacks an arm. It has a story to tell. Once it stood in the synagogue of a Russian town. In the course of forty years, first one Jew, then another, would manage to escape and arrive in Jerusalem. Each took a part of the chair with him, and as they arrived the parts were assembled and the chair was gradually reconstructed. One day the missing arm, too, will arrive, and then the chair will be complete.

IV

OLD WAYS AND NEW

❦

Iᴺ a cultured Jewish home in Jerusalem about 1930 there
lived three intelligent brothers, whose father, E. L. Sukenik,
was Professor of Archaeology in the Hebrew University
there. Professor Sukenik was afterwards to become famous as
the finder of the Dead Sea scrolls. These boys were scouts, who
would spend their holidays with friends roaming the country-
side, when they did not accompany their father on archaeological
excursions, learning from him the history of the mountains
and roads of the Holy Land. Later when they grew up it
became a popular joke in Jerusalem that one worked in
the sky, one between earth and sky, and one under the earth,
the first being an airman, the second an actor, and the third
(the one whom our story is about) an archaeologist like his
father.

He now calls himself Yigal Yadin, having, like many Jews
in Palestine, hebraized his name. Even when young he showed
exceptional promise as an archaeologist; but when his friends
smilingly remarked that his work was 'under the earth' their words
had a double meaning. Yadin's student days were in the years
just before the Second World War, which in Palestine were an
unsettled period. The Arabs were in rebellion, partly against the
British Mandate but mainly against the hundreds of thousands
of Jewish settlers who had arrived there in the course of the last
half century. Determined to frighten the Jews away, the Arabs
would ambush them, set fire to their homes and farms, and
steal their cattle and crops in the night. The Jews reacted by
organizing a secret Home Guard, the *Haganah*—a name

meaning 'Defence'. Haganah operated with weapons that were either home-made or smuggled and trained its men in remote parts, just as did the resistance movements in occupied Europe during the Second World War.

In this volunteer army Yadin displayed such outstanding abilities that in 1948, the year in which the State of Israel was founded, and Haganah was able to function openly as the national defence force, he was appointed its Chief of Staff, perhaps the youngest in the world, for he was only thirty-one. He was the man responsible for drawing up plans for defending Israel against the combined attack of her neighbours. They had counted on crushing the new State in a fortnight and sweeping the Jews into the sea, and all the world expected this to happen. The Arab numerical superiority made it difficult to draw any other conclusion. There were 600,000 Jews, and ranged against them were 40,000,000 Arabs. Moreover, the Israeli army was almost without arms and its opponents had at least some modern equipment. It was another case of David and Goliath, and the Biblical story was in fact re-enacted in what the Israelis call 'the war of miracles'.

It was clear by the autumn of 1948 that the Israelis had the situation well in hand. They had held their positions on the long northern frontier and had captured extensive areas. Things looked less promising in the south, where the Egyptians had occupied the greater part of the Negev, the large area of rocky desert which formed the borderland. Without the Negev Israel is doomed, and consequently Yadin was ordered to recapture it.

By the time he struck in October, Israel had procured modern weapons, buying them up wherever they were to be obtained and flying them in in the dead of night. With grim humour, Yadin called this part of the campaign 'Operation the Ten Plagues of Egypt'. It led to an Egyptian defeat. Beersheba, the largest town in the Negev, was captured. But the frontier district near to Beersheba was still in the hands of the Egyptians, who had erected concrete defensive positions. A frontal attack would have been costly and an encircling movement risky, with the danger of motor vehicles getting bogged down in sand. A way was found—literally 'a way'.

In all the world there were perhaps no more than two or three archaeologists who knew that, 2000 years ago, the Romans had constructed a road running from Egypt up through Palestine, somewhere to the west of the road where the Egyptians had dug themselves in. This road had suffered the same fate as everything else in the country that had once been a 'land flowing with milk and honey'. During centuries of neglect it had fallen into disuse and been buried and forgotten under the drifting sand. One of the archaeologists who knew of this road was the Chief of the Israeli General Staff, and he sent out two eighteen-year-old students to locate it. Israel's future depended on their report. They declared it to be difficult but not impossible. Plans were laid accordingly.

On a late December afternoon (it was Christmas Eve), at a time as near to sunset as possible so as to minimize the risk of air observation, the Israeli columns moved out from Beersheba and drove on to the old road. It is narrow—ancient vehicles were small—but there was just room for tanks and jeeps. But if they missed their course by inches, the wheels on one side would stick hub-deep in the sand. Slowly, cautiously, with all their lights extinguished, the long columns crawled along. They were so near to the Egyptian positions that alert guards would have heard them, but presumably such a risky advance had never occurred to them. It took fifteen hours to cover eighteen miles. And all went well. At dawn on Christmas Day the Israelis crossed the frontier, wheeled, and advanced on the Egyptian rear. Complete surprise was achieved.

'We were at breakfast,' a captured Egyptian colonel said, 'when they jumped through the windows and pointed their rifles at us.'

The battle was soon over, and the surprised troops surrendered. The Negev was in Israeli hands and the road to Cairo lay open.

Twelve years have gone by since that victory and many convulsions have shaken the Middle East since. But the story of that Christmas night will always be remembered: of how an army of modern tanks drove to victory along a road that was 2000 years old. It is the combination of old and new that is so characteristic of what goes on in Israel today.

'Our country is so small,' Yigal Yadin told me, 'that we cannot be content with the ordinary dimensions. We have to use a third—our ancient past. On the eve of the battle of the Nile, Napoleon said to his troops: "Remember that four millennia look down on you." The exhortation to bravery met with the right response, but in that case it was not their own history which inspired the French troops. Modern Israel, however, knows that she has a great history in a land that is now hers once more. Our men stand guard on roads and mountains, in passes and gorges where our forefathers fought before them, and which they know from their reading of the Bible.'

And Yadin went on:

'The landscape has not changed in the last 2000–3000 years; our enemies may have other names, but they are descendants of those who strove to eliminate us in the remote past; the roads they used are the same. Once they came in chariots; now they come in tanks. The difference is not great. Of course everything is more complicated in the jet age, but the principles are still the same. Study the Bible and you will find the same strategic problems. That was something the Egyptian army did not understand; their general staff had only modern tourist maps. Farouk even accused us of unchivalrous warfare; he apparently thought it unfair of us to use roads that were unknown! But we lost 2000 years in this country, and now we are making up for it.'

On my first visit to Israel I asked a friend what books I should find useful. I had expected that I should need ten or twelve works of reference. The reply I got was:

'In Israel you will need only one book. Put that in your pocket. It is the Bible! That is our sacred book, and at the same time it is our national history; in it you will find all you want to know about national customs and festivals. More than that, the Bible is the foundation of practical affairs in our country; we use it as an economic geography and locate copper, iron, and oil with its aid. Furthermore, it teaches us to wage war.'

We shall be returning to the Bible many times in later chapters of this book. Recently, there has been a new illustration of how it can make old new and shed fresh light on past and present. The examples are endless, but let us take Yigal Yadin's latest discovery. After the war the general returned to his archaeology and he is now Professor of Archaeology in Jerusalem, like his father before him. During the last five years he has been leading the great excavations of the ancient town of Hazor.

At hundreds of points in Palestine there are small hillocks, which are obviously not natural formations, because they are conical with round sides and flat tops. A mound of this kind is known as a *tel*, and it indicates the site of a town. Thousands of years ago people settled, built themselves houses, and erected a defensive wall. The town was captured by enemies, who killed the inhabitants and destroyed the town. But the site was a good one, and a later generation would return and build a new town on the ruins of the old. History would repeat itself and one day that, too, would be a ruin. Then another town would grow up, as Phoenix rose from the ashes once again. That is how a *tel* originated.

It presents a challenge to every archaeologist, and one day it is excavated layer by layer and the expert studies it, using modern techniques to date each successive layer by its pottery, coins, lamps, utensils, and plant seeds. One *tel* that has been excavated contains eighteen different towns and has a history of over 4000 years.

In Upper Galilee, at the foot of the mountains nine miles from the Lake of Gennesaret, lay a *tel* which enclosed the town of Hazor; or towns of Hazor, for there had been many, and each had been destroyed by fire and sword. Hazor was a famous town in ancient times. Its name occurs centuries before the Bible, on clay tablets that were preserved in the Egyptian sand, all dating from the nineteenth century before Christ. But the most celebrated are the Tel Amarna finds, a collection of Egyptian public records which contains letters and despatches to Pharaoh from governors and vassals in his far-flung empire, dating from the fourteenth century before Christ. Among them are letters from the King of Hazor.

We also read of Hazor in the Bible, and can follow the history of a succession of towns, all having the same fate, from the capture of Canaan until its subsequent loss. It is not surprising that this town was important. It occupied a key position, on what is said to be the oldest road in the world, one which connects two of the cradles of civilization, the Nile valley and Mesopotamia, the land between the Euphrates and the Tigris. This famous *Via Maris* followed the sea through Palestine (hence its name), turned east through the Valley of Jezreel, and then divided to the north of the Lake of Gennesaret, one branch proceeding eastward to Mesopotamia and the other northward to Syria. Here at this junction, commanding the two most important roads in the area, stood Hazor. The area is still a cornerstone in Israel's defence.

In the period of Israelitic expansion when Joshua conquered the land of Canaan, a decisive battle took place near Hazor, 'by the waters of Merom', which was presumably Lake Huleh. The King of Hazor commanded a defensive league against the Israelites, but the fortunes of war did not favour him. 'And the Lord delivered them into the hands of Israel, who smote them' reads the grim account of the victory in the Book of Joshua. Hazor was taken and destroyed by fire. But the town recovered, and a fresh layer was superimposed on the old one. In the Book of Judges we read of King Jabin of Hazor and General Sisera, who commanded a mighty force of 900 chariots. Yet he too was vanquished, thanks to the inspiration of the prophetess Deborah and the leadership of Barak. Sisera met an ignominious death in the tent of Jael, for while he slept the Israelite woman hammered a tent nail into his temple. King Jabin, too, fell, and once again Hazor was laid waste. Its rebuilder was no less a person than Solomon, the great King being cautious enough to erect forts at various strategic points in his Kingdom. Three of these we know: they are, in addition to Hazor, Megiddo, which controlled the Valley of Jezreel, and Gezer, in the Valley of Ajalon, where the sun stood still for Joshua. Solomon's Hazor also perished, this time for good, in the Assyrian campaign against the Northern Kingdom, when King Tiglath-Peleser overthrew it and carried its people into exile. The account of the disaster in Kings lists Hazor as one of the towns that were destroyed; its king, Pekah, was slain. And so, for 2000 years, the *tel* has stood watch over the ancient city.

Yigal Yadin and his team of archaeologists have stripped the *tel* layer by layer and recovered its hidden treasures. These men are scientists and scholars, not religious zealots bent on proving the historical correctness of the Bible. Nevertheless, their results brilliantly confirm and supplement the Biblical story.

The top, most recent layer of the *tel* presents a shocking picture of destruction; the town had been utterly wiped out by the Assyrians. The layer of ashes is a yard thick, the stones are blackened by fire, and in most places nothing remains but the foundations. Among the debris was a wine-cup bearing the inscription LPQH, which may be interpreted as 'To Pekah'; in short, it belonged to the King who was slain. Beside it was a relief which bore the image of Tiglath-Pileser. Victor and vanquished side by side!

When American archaeologists had excavated Megiddo twenty or thirty years before, they had found a town gate of distinctive construction. When approaching the gate at Hazor, therefore, Yadin made an interesting experiment. It would be fascinating to know, he thought, if Solomon had employed the same architect at both towns, in which case one might expect that the gates would be alike. He accordingly marked off the ground on the same plan as that at Megiddo and his men started digging. 'You will find a gate here that will look like this,' he told them. And there, after two weeks of digging, the gate stood revealed exactly as he had foretold. 'The workmen thought we were magicians,' he told me; 'but when we read

out the account in Kings, they realized how we had known.'
Later on, Yadin demonstrated that the gate at Gezer was of the
same easily recognizable construction, and so was presumably
by the same architect.

The Hazor which was captured by Joshua was a large city
of 40,000 inhabitants. In this layer Mycenaean pottery was
found, a discovery which fixed the date of the Israelite conquest
of Canaan at the thirteenth century before Christ—a very
significant fact. A vast number of other interesting finds have
been made, including stables, casemates for the troops, objects
of fine art, and all manner of utensils. A shrine appears to be
the architectural prototype of Solomon's temple in Jerusalem.

Yadin's work at Hazor is still going on, and perhaps the
most exciting results lie ahead. The archaeologists have now
reached the archives of the old Canaanite kings, and it is not
impossible that they will find there the replies which Pharaoh
sent to the letters from Hazor we know from Tel Amarna. If
so, we shall have a complete file of correspondence 3300 years
old. Yes, indeed, the roads of Israel extend far back into the
mists of time.

Those roads were never forgotten by the people of Israel
during the sixty generations when they wandered on alien paths
that led, if they led anywhere at all, to the stakes of the
Inquisition and the gas chambers of Hitler. Over the centuries
there were some, in each generation, who found the road, if it
was only in order to die under the shade of Mount Zion. Less
than a hundred years ago some words spoken by Isaiah began
to be heard with increasing force: 'Build ye roads, build ye
roads and pave them; clear the paths for my people.' Those who
started it were few in numbers, but the numbers swelled and
soon many were turning as though by instinct towards Zion.
Each left his footprints on the tracks, and the tracks became
paths, the paths roads. A people were going home, dreams were
becoming reality, an old road was being turned into a new one.
It is now possible to see some of the milestones on that road.

The first was erected by Theodor Herzl when he wrote *Der
Judenstaat* in 1896. The next was the Balfour Declaration of

November 2, 1917, which established the legal foundation for
Jewish settlement in Palestine. It is clear that realistic political
considerations led British statesmen to take so sensational a
step. In his memoirs, David Lloyd George describes the pre-
carious situation in which the Allies were placed in 1917, with
the Italian retreat from Caporetto, unsuccessful offensives in
France, and heavy shipping losses due to the unrestricted
U-boat campaign. It was important to enlist the support of
world Jewry by means of a clear demonstration of good will.

Yet more lay in the Declaration than that. Chaim Weizmann,
the Zionist spokesman during the negotiations with the British
Government, which were not always easy, was doubtless right
when he said:

'One of the differences between that time and ours is in the
approach to State problems. The so-called realism of modern
politics is not realism at all, but pure opportunism, lack of
moral stamina, lack of vision, and the principle of living from
hand to mouth. Those British statesmen of the old school, I
have said, were genuinely religious. They understood as a reality
the concept of the Return. It appealed to their tradition and
their faith.'

Balfour was Foreign Secretary in Lloyd George's War
Cabinet, and as such made the famous declaration which bears
his name. The essence is contained in the sentence:

'His Majesty's Government view with favour the establishment in Palestine of a national home for the Jewish people, and
will use their best endeavours to facilitate the achievement of
this object, it being clearly understood that nothing shall be
done which may prejudice the civil and religious rights of
existing non-Jewish communities in Palestine, or the rights and
political status enjoyed by Jews in any other country.'

Protracted negotiations had preceded the declaration and the
Zionists had hoped for more than they actually achieved. What
they wanted was a promise of Palestine as the Jewish national

home; what they got was the promise of 'a' national home. There is a big difference in the two wordings; but even in its restricted form the Balfour Declaration marked a decisive turning-point. Those who sponsored it were conscious that they were offering something big and positive. Balfour called the declaration his greatest achievement, and Lord Robert Cecil, one of the founders of the League of Nations, thought that the idea of a Jewish home in Palestine was as important as that of the League.

The First World War belongs to the past and the published letters, diaries, and memoirs have revealed many hidden motives and manœuvres; doubtless there was more in the declaration than met the eye. Balfour said, a few months later, that in time the Jews would establish a Jewish State in Palestine; that was their own affair, he added, but the British would provide them with the opportunity. The British Government firmly believed that in the tangle of Middle East politics a Jewish State would be their one dependable ally in the long run.

The way ahead seemed to have been charted. In the campaigns of 1917 and 1918 General Allenby conquered the Holy Land. In the peace treaty Turkey ceded Palestine and a British Mandate was set up with the Balfour Declaration as one of its obligations. In 1922 the status was ratified by the fifty-one members of the League of Nations, and Weizmann exchanged friendly notes with Emir Faisal, afterwards King of Iraq, the Arab leader. It is interesting now to recall that T. E. Lawrence, who organized the Arab revolt against the Turks, at that time favoured Jewish immigration into Palestine, in the belief that it would be beneficial to the Arabs. Everything thus seemed to augur a peaceful development. As it soon turned out, the path was to be both steep and stony.

It is one of the ironies of history that the only period since 1920 when there has been peace in Palestine was during the five or six years of the Second World War when the rest of the world was in flames. The years before and after the war were periods of chaos, confusion, and bloodshed. The words of a British statesman, who said that though Palestine was no bigger than an English county its problems were those of a continent, proved to be only too true. There were three powerful forces at work.

Arab national feelings were inflamed by Jewish settlement. The Arab social and political system is feudalistic and anti-quated, in which the vast majority of the people resembles the base of a pyramid surmounted by a few fortunate kings and sheikhs. These rulers saw the modern ideas of Israel as a threat to their interests. There was also the political instability and continual unrest that are endemic in under-developed countries. Here was fertile soil for fanatical nationalism, as well as for those who fish in troubled waters. The consequence was rebellion and Jewish persecution, which flared up repeatedly, especially before 1939.

At the same time, the Jews of Central Europe, threatened by Hitlerism, looked to Palestine for asylum. Successive waves of immigrants multiplied the Jewish population during the thirty years between 1918 and 1948 ten times, from 63,000 to rather more than 600,000. Many of the settlers, nervous already, were driven to desperation when they found that even in the promised land they had to live with a trowel in one hand and a sword in the other. Consequently, they enrolled in the growing terrorist organizations, which ruthlessly avenged broken promises by the British and in relations with the Arabs adopted the policy of an eye for an eye and a tooth for a tooth.

To increase the confusion, the British, who should have been a stabilizing authority, began to give way to Arab demands. The more they yielded, the more the appetite of the Arab leaders increased. The first development took place in 1922, when Transjordan was separated from Palestine. Though these two areas had always been one, the British Government felt constrained to compensate Emir Abdullah for old wrongs. Mr Churchill, the Colonial Secretary at the time, therefore severed the territory to the east of the Jordan, forming the artificial State of Transjordan, later known as Jordan. The climax of British appeasement came in 1939 with the publication of the White Paper by the Chamberlain government. In this it was laid down that the Jewish population in Palestine should not exceed one-third of the total, and that, therefore, only a further 75,000 would be admitted over a period of five years. At the same time, the area where they might obtain land was restricted to a minor part of the country. While the Jews in Europe were moving towards tragedy, the British Government had thus shut them off from their only asylum.

When Labour took up office at the end of the war a radical change in British policy on the Palestine issue was generally expected, for when in opposition it had attacked the Conservative government's approach. It therefore came as a surprise when the Attlee government, with Ernest Bevin as Foreign Secretary, continued the same policy. It even went further and intensified its opposition to the Jews, sometimes employing brutal force. A particularly shocking display of force was the *Exodus* affair, when the British refused to admit a few hundred survivors from German concentration camps, who had tried to land illegally. Their ship *Exodus* was forced to return to the country which held for them such bitter memories.

Palestine now became a major world problem. The tension was intolerable and time and again the country was front-page news. Commission after commission presented report after report. The Middle East is one of the most sensitive centres in world affairs, where the strategic and economic interests of East and West meet in conflict. The problem finally became so involved that the peace of the world was in danger.

When things were at their blackest, two dramatic incidents took place and suggested a possible solution. The British Government suddenly announced that they wished to be relieved of the mandate. The decision was accepted by the United Nations, and on November 29, 1947, the General Assembly resolved, by a two-thirds majority, that Palestine should be divided into an Arab and a Jewish part. Britain abstained from voting, but both the United States and the Soviet Union voted in favour of the proposal. It was the first time since the war that East and West had stood together on an important issue.

The proposal to divide the disputed territory had been made

previously but had met with little enthusiasm; the Arabs were firmly opposed to it and the Jews were doubtful. Their doubt is not surprising when it is remembered that Palestine had already been reduced to a quarter of its original size by the separation of Transjordan, and that the further division would restrict the Jewish part to less than one-eighth. There were also geographical objections from the point of view of the Jews. They were being allotted the eastern part of Galilee, the Valley of Jezreel, the Plain of Sharon between Haifa and Tel Aviv, and most of the Negev. The new Jewish State would resemble a long snake curled along the Mediterranean. Nowhere more than about twelve miles from the nearest frontier, it would be impossible to defend.

Yet Jews everywhere were overjoyed by the United Nations decision. They were at last in sight of their objective—a country of their own. There was dancing and singing among the survivors of Belsen and the internees in Cyprus. Tens of thousands crowded the streets of New York's Riverside East. Jerusalem and Tel Aviv were hives of excitement, the streets packed with singing crowds.

Only Ben-Gurion and his nearest associates were afraid when they thought of the future, fearing, as they did, that war lay ahead.

The final months of British rule proved to be the worst in that troubled country's existence. The British Government had proclaimed May 15, 1948, as the day on which they would hand over control, but they had lost it long before. The Arabs had risen in violent protest against partition, and demonstrations and disturbances shook the country from end to end. Bombs exploded in the cities as Jewish newspaper offices, office buildings, and the Jewish headquarters in Jerusalem were blown up. Jewish terrorists retaliated by blowing up the British Command Headquarters at the King David Hotel in Jerusalem. Fighting back, the Jews built up and trained their illegal army, the Haganah, and succeeded in defending their towns and settlements.

In one respect the Haganah was vulnerable. The settlers had to be protected, yet it was well-nigh impossible to maintain the extended communications that were necessary. The Arabs were masters in the art of ambush and surprise attack, with the result that casualties were heavy. A bitter blow was the attack on a hospital convoy near Jerusalem, when seventy doctors and nurses were shot.

The Arabs were plainly out to prevent partition by a campaign of unrestricted terror. If chaos could be created, the plan would have to be dropped. For a time it looked as if they might achieve their aim. The United States began to waver in her policy, and the whole might have ended where it had begun. For the Jewish leaders, however, the die had been cast; it was now or never.

As the fateful day approached when the British would withdraw the situation grew increasingly ominous. The Arab League States—Egypt, Saudi Arabia, Transjordan, Iraq, Syria, and the Lebanon—mobilized and declared they would invade Palestine immediately the British had left. In Palestine itself each side dug itself in. In fierce battles, both infiltrated into each other's territory—in Jaffa, Haifa, Tiberias, Safad. Then sudden panic came over the Arab populations of these towns and they fled headlong. The Jews had gained a useful respite.

Under Ben-Gurion they had long since made their preparations. Picked men had been trained for the posts that would shortly be vacated by the British, supplies had been purchased and stored, a National Council was set up, and a shadow Cabinet was ready to take over. Coins and postage stamps were ready for issue.

Nevertheless, the prospects looked grim. Moshe Shertok (now Sharett), who was destined to be Foreign Minister, had returned from Washington, bringing the American Government's solemn advice to wait. Golda Myerson (now Meir) had visited King Abdullah in Amman, dressed in Arab clothes, and brought back sinister news from there. The King meant to conquer the whole of Palestine, for which task he would deploy the Arab Legion, the strongest army in the Middle East.

Monastery of St Catherine in Sinai

The Jebel Musa in Sinai, where Moses received the tables

...ising the ...ited Nations ... on the ...za border

Eilat, from the Gulf of Aqaba

The new port of Eilat

The port of Eilat in operation

According to military intelligence, hostile armies were advancing on the frontiers from all sides, and as from May 15th the defenceless city of Tel Aviv would be subjected to heavy bombing.

However, the plans went ahead and the National Council, acting, it would seem, against all reason, decided to proclaim the new State. It appeared to be the only course. The leap into the unknown was duly taken on Friday, May 14, 1948.

There was no feasting on that Sabbath eve; the city was blacked out and no one got much sleep during the night. Journalists, on duty by their radio sets, tuned in to America and from there heard the great news, when at midnight the programme was interrupted for an announcement that the United States Government had recognized the State of Israel *de facto*. President Truman had taken this step twelve minutes after the proclamation by Ben-Gurion. The people of Tel Aviv heard the news the following day.

At six o'clock that morning the sirens wailed in the city. The first Egyptian raid was taking place. The war had started.

At the point where the River Jordan leaves the Lake of Gennesaret and flows south, there settled, over half a century ago, a group of Jewish colonizers, the founders of the celebrated settlement of Deganya. It was an inhospitable region 600 feet below sea-level, in summer oppressively hot, swampy and fever-infested. Deganya has been called 'the mother of the *kibbutzim*', for it was there that the first collective settlement was established. The young pioneers were successful in taming the area, and Deganya today is a delightful place of lush sub-tropical scenery. The river flows beneath overhanging trees, the fever has been banished; there are large banana plantations, fertile fields, and healthy cows. All is prosperity and peace.

Yigal Yadin and his staff expected things to happen here. To the south of the lake two rivers and three frontiers meet; flowing westward into the Jordan, the River Yarmuk forms the frontier between Syria and the Kingdom of Jordan, and Israel borders on both of these countries at the confluence of the rivers. This was where Yadin's third dimension came in. In ancient times the road from Damascus to Samaria crossed the River Jordan here, almost on the site of present-day Deganya, forming a through road into the Holy Land. Among the enemies who made use of it was Benhadid, the Aramaean King of Damascus, which is the capital of modern Syria. In the ninth century B.C., Benhadid attacked King Ahab, whom we know from the Bible for his marriage to Jezabel. Benhadid calculated that the God of Israel was a mountain god, and that therefore he would be more successful if he attacked in the plain. Battle was joined in the Jordan Valley, to the south of the Lake of Gennesaret; yet in spite of his prevision Benhadid was defeated. The wars are fully recorded in Kings; and knowing their Bible, the Israeli army leaders made preparations for a stand on this historic site.

The attack duly came and peaceful Deganya found itself in the thick of the fighting when Syrian troops advanced and shelled it. On May 20th, the Syrian general, thinking the fruit ready for the picking, sent his troops into the attack under a screen of gunfire. It was not expected that there would be much defence, and indeed the settlers had little enough to defend themselves with. Forty of them lay entrenched with the only forty rifles which the settlement possessed, along with a few Molotov cocktails: bottles of petrol containing a fuse which explodes the charge when the bottle is smashed. Clearly, tanks could not be stopped by rifle fire, and they crashed through the barriers towards the houses. Deganya seemed lost.

Suddenly, two of the defenders got up and threw their Molotov cocktails, and both of these hit their targets. The foremost tank burst into flames; one of the crew perished in the flames, and the rest were shot as they tried to escape. This was too much for the Syrians: at the sight of the disaster which had befallen their companions the surviving tanks turned and fled. The attack had been repulsed, the Jordan Valley saved.

The two Israelis were ordinary civilians and neither had ever seen a tank or handled a gun before. Perhaps they hardly realized what they had done. But the burnt-out tank stands at the entrance to Deganya now, where it forms a monument to a turning-point in the history of modern Israel.

The battle that has just been described was one of many, and it is typical of the early stages of the war in 1948. Having studied this war and visited the battlefields, as well as talked to hundreds of men and women who took part, I can confidently assert that the Israelis held out almost without arms against tanks, guns, and aircraft—and yet won.

In truth, the situation could hardly have been more desperate. The Egyptian army, advancing northward through the Negev, calculated on reaching Tel Aviv and Jerusalem. Syrian and Lebanese troops struck southward through Galilee. In the centre the situation was even more critical. Here King Abdullah's Arab Legion, with units of Iraqi troops, threatened Israel's 'waistline', the narrow corridor, only twelve miles across, in the Plain of Sharon. If they had broken through, Israel would have been cut in two. The Arabs controlled the air space and could bomb any target they chose.

After the first week, however, the position gradually began to turn. The first supplies started to arrive by air, especially from Czechoslovakia; and in defiance of ordinary military principles, the Israelis attacked wherever the enemy was strongest, for that was where there were most weapons to be captured.

There was one black spot, however; Jerusalem was besieged and its fate hung in the balance. In the centre of the Old Town a small Orthodox community defended itself for as long as there was any hope. The New Town, which had been founded fifty to sixty years earlier and now had 100,000 inhabitants, also defended itself with all it had. The biggest problem was the one of supplies: arms, petroleum, food, and especially water. Water has always been a problem for Jerusalem, for the city stands 2500 feet above sea-level. In olden times the people caught the rain in cisterns; but this is inadequate nowadays, and so supplies are piped from the coastal plains. The Arabs had cut these supplies. Cistern water was rationed to a minimum.

With sardonic humour, they said: 'First we drink it, then we wash in it, and finally we use it for cooking.'

Haganah succeeded in opening a road through the mountains of Judaea. After violent fighting an old Roman fort, Kastel, on the top of a commanding height, was captured, and gradually the road was cleared as far as Bab el Wad, from where there is an unrestricted view across the plain. That seemed to be the limit; for the road to Jerusalem passed through Latrun, a town which proved to be impregnable. Time and again Haganah launched an assault against it, but was beaten off with heavy losses. Latrun was a lock which could neither be picked nor forced. There was only one alternative: to build a new road.

Scouts were sent out to reconnoitre. Groping their way through the mountains, along wadis and ancient camel tracks, they made contact, at dawn, with outposts on the Jerusalem front. They had proved that it was possible to reach the capital by another route. Accordingly, sappers set to work both at Tel Aviv and Jerusalem on a new road, working silently because they were within range of the Arab guns. After weeks of toil the two parties linked up, and the convoys began driving into Jerusalem with their badly needed supplies.

The new road saved Jerusalem but provided no more than an emergency relief. Plans were made for a permanent asphalt road; and as the rainy season approached, the work was speeded up. There was only eight weeks in which to complete a 25-mile road in difficult mountain country. All the young men had already been called up, and so the workers consisted of middle-aged men, schoolboys, disabled persons, some devout Jews wearing earlocks. In the hot sun and on cold nights they worked against time and succeeded in completing their task. The result was a good solid road which now links Jerusalem with the rest of the country, while a pipeline alongside it supplies the city with water. New settlements were founded close to the road for defensive purposes; and it is known as 'Bravery Road'. At the start of the road is an obelisk bearing the inscription: 'If I forget thee, O Jerusalem, may my right hand wither.'

For four weeks the fighting swayed to and fro; but finally the United Nations intervened and on June 11th the first truce took effect. The Arabs' best chance had been to gain a swift decision, and Abdullah had counted on this. According to his time-table, Haifa should have been taken in five days, Jerusalem and Tel Aviv in ten, whereupon Abdullah would have been crowned in Jerusalem king of the united territories of Transjordan and Palestine. His plans were frustrated by the stubborn resistance, and when the truce came the Arabs were on the defensive. There were several reasons for this. For one thing, Israel was now receiving a steady flow of modern arms, and, for another, the Arabs were hampered by long lines of communications, as well as by internal dissension. Most of their men were mercenaries, fighting in a cause they knew little about and hoping for easy loot. The Israelis, on the other hand, were fighting for hearth and home, for their very survival. Theirs was the spirit that had inspired the Son of a Star and his men in the last war by the Jewish people on the Biblical battlefields 2000 years ago. Once again it had been demonstrated that an army's morale is more important than the arms which it bears, even now in a war of modern machines.

The United Nations strove at Lake Success to find a solution to the problem; and Count Folke Bernadotte, who had been appointed mediator, recommended an extension to the truce. This Israel accepted, but the Arabs rejected it. The war therefore broke out again on July 9th, and this time at once took a disastrous turn for the Arabs. Israel went over to the attack, and in the course of a few days the front became fluid. Lydda, with one of the main airports of the Middle East, was captured, together with the neighbouring town of Ramleh. Haganah took the offensive in the north and flung the Arabs back. Nazareth and all Galilee fell into Israeli hands. The new Israeli air force, going into action for the first time, raided Cairo, Amman, and Damascus. The hotly disputed town of Latrun was about to fall to Haganah, and at Jerusalem the Arab League was in full retreat, followed by thousands of Arab refugees. At this crucial moment the war was called off; the Arab States had agreed to

Bernadotte's proposals for a further truce. Ben-Gurion then sounded the cease-fire, though it meant the sacrifice of the Holy City.

In the midst of this struggle for life and death the new-born State was convulsed by two crises, both of them connected with Jewish terrorists. *Irgun Zwai Leumi* (the name means People's Military Organization), together with the Stern group, had waged a private war against the British and the Arabs. Irgun had blown up the King David Hotel and afterwards hanged two British sergeants in retaliation for the execution of two of their own men. Ben-Gurion had always given the terrorists a wide berth, but during the war they had of course stood shoulder to shoulder.

Up to a point only, it should be added. Soon after midsummer, news had arrived that a large ship was on its way to Israel with arms and volunteers from America and Europe. The operation had been organized and paid for by Irgun. Ben-Gurion at once demanded that the cargo should be surrendered, and when Irgun refused there was a bitter quarrel between them. When the rebels still would not yield, Ben-Gurion ordered their ship to be sunk. Then, at the last moment, Irgun gave in and civil war was averted. From long experience Ben-Gurion knows the fatal Jewish tendency to waste energies on internecine quarrels, and he was determined that unity should this time be preserved. It was one of those difficult decision which statesmen sometimes have to make.

Worse things were to follow. On September 17th a tragedy occurred which could well have cost Israel her existence. Count Folke Bernadotte was passing through an outer suburb of Jerusalem on his way to negotiations when his path was barred by a jeep in which were troops in Israeli uniform. One of the men fired his tommy gun through the window of the Count's car and killed both Folke Bernadotte and Colonel Serot, his French *aide*.

This was the Bernadotte who, displaying outstanding initiative, had freed thousands of prisoners from German concentration camps in the final stages of the Hitlerite war. As the United

Nations mediator he had not been popular in Israel; his proposals appeared unfavourable to the Jews, who suspected him of bias. He had now been murdered, and by Jews. A chill fear settled on the country. No better way could have been found to destroy Israel than to assassinate this highly respected man in the Holy City by men wearing Israeli uniforms.

Unfortunately, the murderers got away. As far as it was possible to establish, they were gangsters remotely connected with the Stern group, but there are mysterious features in the case which have not been finally cleared up. Once more, then, the future of Israel hung by a thread. A wave of anger passed through the world. It seemed that there was anarchy in Israel, with the Government powerless to maintain law and order.

Once more Ben-Gurion acted ruthlessly: the terrorist organizations were immediately dissolved. The crisis passed without any of the fatal consequences which had been feared. All unprejudiced observers were agreed that the murder could not have been the work of responsible Israelis, and confidence was gradually restored.

The war came to an end. By means of 'Operation the Ten Plagues of Egypt' and the surprise campaign along the Roman road, Haganah succeeded in clearing the Negev. By the end of 1948 Israel was in control on all fronts and the Arab countries were forced to conclude a truce. On the anniversary of the foundation of the State on May 14, 1949, Israel was admitted to membership of the United Nations. The new road had led to the destination.

Between Bethlehem and Hebron Jewish settlers had founded a settlement to which they had given the name Kfar Etzion. Isolated as it was from other settlements, it had been surrounded at the beginning of May 1948 by large Arab forces. There was no means either of breaking out or of getting relief, and the settlers resolved to defend themselves to the last cartridge. By the ninth day they had no more ammunition left, and so Kfar Etzion was wiped out. At that time everyone in Israel would ask: 'What is the latest news from Kfar Etzion?'

On the ninth day a prominent politician (an atheist) entered Haganah's headquarters in Tel Aviv and asked the regulation question:

'What's the latest news from Kfar Etzion?'

A telegraphist seated at his instrument replied:

'I am just receiving the *last* news from Kfar Etzion.'

And as a death-like silence fell on the room they heard the telegraph tick out the final dispatch. In Hebrew it went:

'*Shmah Israel, Adonai Elohenu, Adonai ahad.*'

It is the great Jewish creed, which is said three times a day throughout life and is the last speech of the dying:

'Hear Israel, the Lord our God; the Lord is One.'

Describing this scene afterwards, the politician said:

'At that moment my world collapsed in ruins. I had thought that the only things which exist are those that can be counted, weighed, and measured. In a flash I saw that life is controlled by invisible powers.'

V

THE SCORPION'S STING

꧁꧂

THE scene was Faluja, a village in southern Palestine; the time, the end of December 1948. Faluja was the one base in Palestine, except for Gaza, that the Egyptians has succeeded in holding. Israeli armoured troops had routed the Egyptian army in Sinai, but the Faluja pocket still held out. A crack Sudanese regiment defended it, and after the truce was able to march out unbeaten.

In a wet trench a thirty-year-old Egyptian captain clenched his fists in impotent despair. Faluja was under fire from Israeli batteries, and the shells from the Egyptian guns did not explode—they were dummies, the ammunition factory had swindled. The man responsible for this corruption was King Farouk. The captain's name was Abdel Gamal Nasser. Abdel means 'God's Servant', and Gamal 'Handsome'.

In this gloomy situation one of his fellow-officers exclaimed: 'Gamal, the front isn't here, it's in Cairo.'

Three or four years later Nasser had established the Cairo front. With a group of young officers—the *Junta*—and with the ageing Colonel Mohammed Naguib for cover, he struck, and King Farouk went into the exile he so richly deserved. Naguib was soon discarded, and Nasser, content with the rank of lieutenant-colonel, is the President of Egypt.

The modest rank is characteristic of the man and his régime. It has been his deliberate policy to establish a position the direct opposite of the luxury of Farouk. Nasser still lives, with his wife and five sons, in an unpretentious bungalow at Abbasiya, the military district of Cairo, and likes to stress his humble origins as a 'son of the people'.

He was born in 1918, in a dusty village in Upper Egypt. His father was a post-office clerk and the family belonged to the lower middle class which for thousands of years has been exploited by pashas and beys. Small wonder that from childhood he harboured an inferiority complex and hated the Establishment. At his mother's wish, young Nasser studied law. As a student he took part enthusiastically in political debates, demonstrations, and street fighting against the ruling class and the British who were in control. By an unexpected chance he was able to enter the military academy, where he was trained by British officers and hated them for their superiority and contemptuous attitude to the Egyptian army. Soon he was a captain, one of the most promising of his class. His bravery in the Palestine war earned for him the nickname 'Lion of Faluja'. His brother officers regarded him as their future leader.

In his early forties, Nasser is a big, heavily built man, but surprisingly fit and agile. Handsome and charming, with curly hair greying at the temples and a hooked nose, he wears a small moustache and when he smiles, as he frequently does, displays a set of regular white teeth. His eyes are brown and piercing, his voice soft and pleasant. Nasser is aware of his charm and can radiate a personal magnetism when he chooses. But those who know him know also that the blandness conceals tenacity. Nasser, too, is a born intriguer. 'I have been a conspirator for so long that I suspect everybody surrounding me,' he has said. There is a cat-like quality about him; also in the sense that he has always managed to fall on his feet. In his dealings with Westerners his method is one of charming moderation; he has even hinted that personally he bears no hostility to Israel and has to say the opposite in deference to public opinion. On occasion he will lie blatantly. When Pineau, the French Foreign Minister, called on him, Nasser gave his word of honour as an officer that Egypt was not aiding the rebels in Algeria. A few days later Pineau obtained proof that he had been deceived— and never forgave the deception.

Nasser is no master of eloquence. He is a monotonous and repetitive speaker and when excited will drop into his local dialect—an unpardonable offence in the eyes of educated Arabs. No one is such an easy prey to words when they flow euphoniously as the Arab, yet only on one occasion has Nasser succeeded in moving his audience to real enthusiasm. This was the announcement of the nationalization of the Suez Canal, when he could scarcely get the words out for the hysterical laughter that was choking him. But he knows the power of words, especially with people who are mainly illiterate. No popular leader owes so much of his influence to the radio as he does; the population of every Arab country listens to the flow of delirious words from Cairo. It would be an exaggeration to call Nasser a new Hitler, but he has a number of small Goebbels's about him and their propaganda has consolidated his power among the Arab nations. Many former Gestapo and ss officers, now wanted as war criminals, have found an asylum in Cairo, where they live under assumed Moslem names and engage in espionage and anti-Jewish propaganda.

In July 1952 the Junta won complete control and found itself faced with tremendous problems. Social differences in Egypt are appalling. Millions of fellahs live on the borderline of starvation, racked by diseases—malaria, dysentry, trachoma, bilherzia (intestinal worms), and cholera—on a scale inconceivable in Europe. Even so the population is increasing at a rate faster than social progress can maintain. The present population is 24,000,000, and the number increases by nearly 500,000 a year. So extreme is the overpopulation that in the northern delta of the Nile there are 10,000 inhabitants to the square mile.

With a dynamic energy which impressed this naturally indolent people the new rulers embarked upon a programme of reforms. Though quite inexperienced they tackled corruption, introduced land reforms, studied new means of employment, and promised social progress and education for all. Undoubtedly the intentions were honourable, but the results so far have been meagre. Not even 'Nasser's pyramid', the great Assuan dam, will be capable of feeding the millions of new mouths at the end of the ten years which it is planned that it will take.

This is where the tragedy of Nasser's career begins. Like many dictators before him he encountered insoluble domestic problems and was tempted to divert attention from them by winning easy victories of foreign policy. And it is a remarkable fact that the officer who never won a battle has achieved a succession of unbelievable victories over Powers that were superior to him in strength, and has been halted only by smaller ones.

His policy has been empirical all along; it was only after he had gained power that he gave his ideas shape. In the *Philosophy of the Revolution*, a volume of lectures, he comes to the conclusion that he is destined to be the new Saladin, a successor to the Arab ruler who, 800 years ago, defeated the Crusaders. He envisages *Al Umma al Araba* (Arab Unity), a united Arab nation that would extend from the Atlantic to the Persian Gulf, from Morocco to Iraq. He sees himself in the role of the hero whom the Arabs for centuries have sought in vain. A continuous propaganda campaign over the air has been dinning this into the ears of the Arabs day and night, for years. The propaganda is backed by action. 'The political murder seemed to me a necessary means to the end we have set ourselves,' Nasser has candidly declared. We shall return to this later.

Nasser is a dangerous gambler. The secret of his diplomacy is in fact no secret at all: he has simply discovered that it is profitable to play one opponent off against the other, and he has got away with it. The interests of Britain and the United States in the Middle East had long been opposed. Nasser gambled on the friendship of the United States, and in 1954 the American Government persuaded Britain to evacuate the Suez base, whereupon Nasser was able to claim that he had abolished the last remnants of colonialism in Egypt. Elsewhere he exploited the differences between Britain and France. There were even greater possibilities in the Cold War between East and West. Egypt found herself being wooed by both. But when Russia came into the picture, Nasser arrived at the crossroads.

Since the time of Peter the Great Russian aspirations have turned in three directions—west, east, and south. In the west the front has been consolidated along the Iron Curtain, in the east along the Pacific coast. To the south, however, all is still flux. Here there are troubled waters still for fishing in. The Western Powers, realizing the danger, made a move to avert it by erecting a 'northern wall' in the Baghdad Pact, embracing Turkey, Iraq, Iran, Pakistan, and Britain. (For tactical reasons the United States preferred to remain an associated Power.) Iraq, proud that she was the first Arab country to be invited, gladly joined. It was the intention eventually to admit the other Arab States one by one. But Egypt resented the fact that Iraq had been invited first; while Farouk had visions of his own country as the major factor in the Middle East, Nasser has followed him in this aspect of his policy.

Nasser's daring counter move was the arms agreement with Russia, made known in September 1955, whereby Russia, through the Czech Skoda works, supplies Egypt with modern arms in return for Egyptian cotton, which she buys at bargain prices. The pact came as a shock both to the West and to Israel, the latter being well aware that she would be the first victim. The initial effect of the agreement was a flow of instructors into Egypt from behind the Iron Curtain; without them Egypt could not have used the new equipment. As time went on the agreement applied not only to military equipment but also to railway material and engineering projects, the most recent of which has been the Assuan dam. Already there are many Russians and Czechs in key Egyptian posts. This is the usual Communist method of gaining a foothold. It looked as if Nasser had chosen the East.

It was not so obvious as it looked, however. Nasser is a religious man, a good Moslem who says his daily prayers, and the Communist régime is godless. When he visited the Soviet Union he was shocked by the atheism. Here there is a gulf between Moscow and Cairo which cannot be bridged. What is more, the Kremlin is by no means eager to seize political control. The form of government is not its prime concern; the

Soviet Union has before reached agreement with its enemies, as witness the Molotov-Ribbentrop pact. What the Kremlin wants is influence. The fruit will fall of itself when it is ripe.

Nasser has played a dangerous game and will go down in history as the man who opened the floodgates of the Middle East to the Russians. While he traded with Russia he banned the Communist Party. Wishing, no doubt, that he were rid of the Russians, he repeatedly complained to Western diplomats that they had forced him into it.

The Western Governments watched Nasser's balancing act with growing irritation. Then suddenly in the summer of 1956 John Foster Dulles announced that the United States had withdrawn her offer to finance the Assuan dam. It was a stunning blow to Nasser, but he was soon on his feet again. He immediately proclaimed the nationalization of the Suez Canal; this would provide him with the means to build his dam. But there were other developments which Nasser had not reckoned with. What happened in London and Paris will be discussed later, but on the other side of the Sinai desert Israel had long been watching the trend in Egypt. She knew that no matter how much the Arab States might quarrel among themselves, there was one thing on which they saw eye to eye: the hope of avenging the defeat of 1948 and destroying Israel. Perhaps the hour of reckoning was at hand.

British policy had given birth to the Kingdom of Jordan; the British had needed a bastion in the Middle East and Trans-jordan, as it was originally named, was the result. It was an artificial country, without natural ties of history, nationhood, or economic background. Jordan is an empty desert and its frontiers are straight lines drawn on sand. Only five per cent of its area is under cultivation; there are no industries, and none of the oil which is so profitable to her neighbours.

The British bequeathed Jordan the romantic figure of Glubb Pasha, whose English name is General John Bagot Glubb. Glubb Pasha was appointed head of the Arab Legion, a force of 15,000 men armed and trained by the British, and the only

Arab army which emerged more or less unbeaten from the war with Israel.

Glubb Pasha became to the Arabs an Arab. He spoke their language, wore their dress, slept in their tents, rode on their camels; it is even said that this British officer became so much an Arab that he scratched himself out of politeness, just as Arabs have to do for other reasons. While the command of the Legion was in Glubb's hands the British could rest assured. But it was a costly insurance policy, for the country was subsidized to the tune of £20,000,000 a year.

It was fortunate for the British that Abdullah, the first King of Jordan, remained their faithful vassal. A scion of the ancient Hashemite line of kings, he was descended in the thirty-eighth generation from the great-grandfather of the Prophet. From time immemorial the family had resided at Mecca until driven into exile by King Ibn Saud. The British, protecting the defeated Hashemites, placed Abdullah on the throne of Jordan and his brother Faisal on the Iraqi throne. For as long as Abdullah remained king in Amman there was peace. This shrewd ruler knew where his interests lay, and often gained British support for their promotion.

In the Palestine war the Legion occupied central Palestine, the Arab triangle formed by the Old Town of Jerusalem, Jericho, Bethlehem, Hebron, and the Biblical Samaria, and Abdullah annexed it. The acquisition proved to be a dangerous one, for not only were Abdullah's allies envious of him, the district was full of refugees from Israel—desperate characters who thought only of revenge and had often threatened death to the royal house. Abdullah indeed was their first important victim, for he was assassinated in Jerusalem. He had been the only Arab ruler to realize that Israel had come to stay and that it was necessary to seek an accord with this new neighbour. No sooner was it rumoured in Cairo, that Abdullah was negotiating with Israel however, before sentence had been passed on him. One summer day in 1951 as he entered the Al Aqsa mosque in Jerusalem a man sprang forward from his hiding-place behind a pillar and shot him. His bodyguard fell

frightened to the floor, and the only person who made any
attempt to save him was a fifteen-year-old boy, his grandson
Hussein.

Hussein is now King of Jordan. In the early years of his
reign this boy king (only seventeen when he came to the throne)
was regarded as a nonentity. Glubb Pasha was his guardian,
and the two could be seen walking together in the garden of the
royal palace, the well-behaved boy holding the older man's
hand as though in symbolical obedience. Incidentally, Hussein
would drive his car at 150 miles an hour on the runway of
Amman's airport, and while visiting Los Angeles once broke
the sound barrier in a Lockheed Starfighter.

The young King proved to be more capable than anyone had
dreamt of, more than was to the liking of the astute intriguer
in Cairo. He had been the only courageous person when the
bullets had whistled in the mosque and his grandfather had
been killed; and his courage has more than once saved his own
life and throne. Hearing, in 1955, of an officers' plot against
him, he sprang into his car and drove straight off for army
headquarters at Zerga, where he entered unarmed and ordered
the rebels to be arrested. His commands were obeyed.

A corner of Abdullah's diplomatic cloak must have fallen on
his grandson. Hussein's reign has been a perilous dance on the
edge of a knife. The Communists had a large following among
his subjects in Palestine, and the influence of Nasser is wide and
deep. Cairo radio stirs up emotions in refugee camps and outside them. The first serious crisis arose when the pro-Western
government of Jordan was on the point of joining the Baghdad
pact. Nasser sensed the danger and, with the King of Saudi
Arabia, bribed the Amman mob to commit violence. The capital
was thrown into a turmoil; British and American offices were
destroyed; the cry of 'Long live Nasser!' went up; and the
assassins made for the King.

At a General Election the Palestinian party gained a majority.
This party favoured a pan-Arab policy in alliance with Syria
and Egypt, and the King moved in their direction. To yield has
always been the only course open to him, but there is a limit and

time and again he has succeeded in asserting some degree of independence for himself and his Kingdom. His success so far has been in the nature of a miracle. Two factors have saved him: his personal popularity (though with a volatile people this can be unreliable); and the support of the Bedouins, who at critical moments rally round him at the palace.

Jordan, however, never joined the Baghdad pact, and in the spring of 1956 the King went so far as to dismiss Glubb Pasha, giving him twenty-four hours in which to quit the country he had served for thirty-six years. The departure was so rapid that Glubb had barely time to pack. At the same time Jordan terminated her alliance with Britain. Egypt and Saudi Arabia guaranteed the subsidies, and the guarantee was afterwards assumed by the United States. In October 1956 Jordan subscribed to the Egyptian-Syrian defence pact under joint Egyptian command.

Ever since 1948 the fires had smouldered along Israel's extensive frontiers. In October 1956 they looked like flaring up. Would there be open war again?

'Israel is a cancer in the flesh of the Arab people.'

These words were spoken by Mohammed Naguib, the man whom Nasser thrust aside. There is no mistaking the hatred which they express; and Naguib was not the only prominent Arab who spoke bitterly and threateningly. Azzam Pasha, the secretary-general of the Arab League, speaking at the outbreak of the war, declared the war aims in the following clear-cut terms:

'This will be a war of extermination; a massacre so great that it will be remembered like those of the Mongols and the Crusaders.'

And the young King Ibn Saud said, as he ascended his father's throne at Riadh:

'Our only course is to root out Israel. If necessary we must sacrifice 10,000,000 of our 50,000,000 Arabs in order to continue to live in greatness and honour.'

Reporting the King's speech in the Knesset, the Israeli Parliament, Ben-Gurion drily observed:

'I should be interested to know if King Ibn Saud includes himself among the 10,000,000.'

So intense is the hatred and bitterness that when I heard these words repeated in one of the Arab countries, I could hardly believe my ears.

I have already said that passions ran high in the refugee camps. These, indeed, have long been a difficult issue—as well as a ghastly human problem—that for twelve years has defied solution.

The stream of refugees started at Haifa, where there was heavy fighting between Haganah and Arab legionaries who had crossed over into the town. Fighting with all the courage of despair, the Jews succeeded in gaining the upper hand. They offered a truce, which was refused. Instead there was a mass flight. Thousands of the Arab inhabitants of Haifa took the roads which led north or, hurrying down to the port, sailed off in small vessels. The Jewish authorities did what they could to allay the panic. Loudspeaker vans touring the streets of the Arab quarters throughout the day broadcast offers of peace and civic rights. It was all of no avail. Of the 63,000 Arab inhabitants of Haifa, nearly 60,000 fled. The leaders went first and the rest followed them.

The flight from Haifa had far-reaching consequences. It made a profound impression throughout the Arab districts of Palestine; and it was infectious. A mass psychosis seemed to have the whole Arab population in its grip. After Haifa came Jaffa, Tiberias, Safad, and many villages. It cannot be denied that Jewish terrorists did what they could in order to make things worse. Irgun Zwai Leumi was guilty of an outrage when one of its units captured the village of Dir Yassin near Jerusalem and wantonly murdered 250 inhabitants, including many women and children. Reports of this crime flew round the country. Afterwards, whenever Jewish troops entered an Arab village the villagers would cry 'Dir Yassin' and, leaving all behind them, would flee in terror along the nearest road.

Apart from this isolated case, there is no evidence that the mass flight was deliberately provoked. The Arab High Commission, under the chairmanship of the ex-Mufti of Jerusalem, Haj Amin el Husseini, who was a friend of the late Adolf Hitler and an implacable enemy of the Jews, gave the order for the evacuation of Arabs from the Jewish areas of Palestine. The ex-Mufti had reckoned with bitter fighting and violent air raids and tank warfare, and he wanted to have his hands free. He reasoned that the campaign would be easier if the Arab troops were allowed to stand alone against the Jews, who were to be 'thrown into the sea'. All were sure of victory, and the evacuees were told that they would be able to return home in a few weeks' time. Those who did not obey the order, it was pointed out, would be regarded as traitors and could expect the worst. The British, for their part, made no effort to check the hysteria. Indeed, the flight fitted in with their own plans. The result would be a vacuum behind the Jewish lines; for under the Mandate thousands of Arabs had held public employment in the post office, on the railways, in the water department, and in offices generally, and the sudden departure of all these people would bring chaos and confusion. Neither the Arabs nor the British, however, reckoned with the possibility that the Jews had foreseen such an emergency and had freshly trained men waiting to take over the posts as soon as they became vacant.

It is necessary to know something of Arab mentality in order to understand how this mass hypnosis could arise and bring about such disastrous results. These handsome, charming, and friendly people were a picturesque element in Palestine. But one did not have to know very much about them in order to realize how backward they were. Poor and ignorant, they submitted willingly to the archaic feudal system and obeyed their leaders in everything. Their whole environment was out of date—their houses, their fields, their implements. Tribes and families clung together and blood feuds and strange traditions flourished among them. Never in any hurry, they dreamed away their lives remote from every reality as we understand it. Time, to them, was no object; their Oriental outlook was reflected in the saying 'A day is as a thousand years, and a thousand years as a day.' When such people are cajoled and threatened there is little wonder if violence is the result. The responsibility belongs to those who initiated the flight.

The number of those who fled from Israel has been hotly disputed and sometimes fantastic figures have been cited. It cannot have been more than the number actually living in the Israeli part of Palestine at the time; that is, between 550,000 and 600,000. And there were 170,000 still there when it was all over. Still, it was a big enough number even so, and it involved many human tragedies. The United Nations provided shelter, food, and clothing, as well as education and health services. The fact that there are nearly a million inmates of the camps proves that not all of them can be refugees. Truth to tell, in the two areas where there are most—Jordan and Gaza— many poor Arabs laid false claims to refugee status. Food and services may be limited in the camps, but are better there than they are outside. That is the attraction, and many so-called refugees have been admitted. There are various other facts which should be borne in mind. Sir Winston Churchill said that between 1924 and 1939 the Arab population of Palestine rose by 300,000. Many of this number were attracted to Palestine by the economic prosperity which the Jews had created. It is an exaggeration to regard them as real citizens of Israel; rather their flight must be considered a return home. It is only fair to remember that after 1948 the Arab States compelled 500,000 Jews to abandon their homes and take refuge, empty-handed, in Israel.

Argument, however, is fruitless; what the refugees want is re-settlement, and there is room and a crying need for more people in the countries which took them in. With international assistance, extensive areas could be made sufficiently fertile to enable them to get a living. The Arab Governments, however, continue to bar the way by insisting that Israel must be crushed and the refugees sent 'home'. As such a prospect is remote in the extreme, the unfortunate refugees are now no more than pawns in a game of power politics, with human lives being sacrificed on the altar of political prestige. Israel refuses to take them back, but is willing, as part of a general settlement, to pay compensation for property left behind and to accept members of broken families. She cannot admit the refugees *en bloc*. They have been systematically drilled into hating her and to take them in now would be tantamount to admitting a fifth column.

The war of 1948 ended in a cease-fire. Usually, a cease-fire marks a transition from war to peace. In 1949 only the blackest of pessimists would have thought that it would be more than six months, or a year at the most, before peace was signed. Yet over twelve years have now gone by, and still there is no peace between Israel and the Arabs. Time out of number the Security Council has been convened to debate further outbreaks of hostility. It has adopted resolutions and declarations of regret and disapproval; it has despatched fact-finding commissions, superseded officers, discussed fresh measures, given advice and instructions *ad infinitum*. All in vain. Once more the problems of this sensitive corner of the world have reached deadlock. Every new attempt to find a settlement runs counter to the stony hatred of the Arab States for Israel, the country they do not really know. Their single aim is to remove her from the scroll of nations. There has been no peace treaty, only a cease-fire; so that, technically, the war is still on, though it varies in intensity. At times it is only a cold war, but at others it is hot. Let us take a look at the cold war first.

Israel is the subject of an economic blockade aimed at strangling her. Up to 1948 there was busy trade between Palestine and her neighbours. Now the frontiers are enclosed by the barbed wire of hate. When for the first time I stood by one of the frontier posts, a friend hastened to warn me:

'Take care! You'll die if you cross the border.'

The blockade is world-wide. There is an office in Cairo that is busily engaged in severing the links between Israel and other countries. International firms trading with Israel are black-listed; air and shipping companies which maintain connections with Israel may not use Arab airfields or ports. The Dutch firm of Philips, the British Shell, the Lambretta scooter factory in Italy, the Renault works in France removed plant from Israel to avoid reprisals by the Arab countries, whose markets are too valuable to lose. West Germany was violently attacked when she paid indemnities to Israel; but in this case the Federal Republic remained unmoved.

There are two points where the blockade is painfully evident. The Suez Canal has been closed to Israeli shipping since 1948; and at the beginning of 1958 the carriage of Israeli cargoes in ships of other nationalities was also blocked. For eight months the Danish ship Inge Toft lay in Port Said with a cargo of Israeli cement and potash. Under international law this is illegal; the Suez Convention of 1888 lays it down that, in peace and in war, the ships of all countries shall pass without hindrance. The Security Council has declared the blockade illegal. Mr Dag Hammarskjöld made repeated representations in Cairo. But every attempt to get Egypt to respect her inter-national obligations has failed. The blockade of the Gulf of Aqaba, which lasted until 1956, was a serious blow to Israel. Here she is building a new port. Haifa is the gateway to the west, and in the same way Eilat, at the head of the Gulf of Aqaba, is the gateway to the east. But immediately after the 1948 war Egypt built, at Sharm el Sheik, at the southern tip of Sinai, a fortress which bars the way to Israeli ships.

Then there is the hot war. Israel's long, open frontiers, some 600 miles long, are a serious temptation. Bands of smugglers would cross the Negev from Jordan at night loaded with the coveted drug hashish for the Egyptian black market; refugees lusting for revenge also slipped across the borders. Serious clashes became frequent. The Arabs, cunning at ambushes, have attacked buses, fired on solitary field workers, and stolen cattle and implements. The Egyptian army turned murder into a system when patrols of regular officers known as *fedayin* were trained at Gaza. The name means 'suicides', and originally the *fedayin* were idealistic students, ready to sacrifice their lives against the British at the Suez base. When the base was evacuated the *fedayin* turned their attentions on Israel, and by this time the quality had deteriorated, as it had been found difficult to fill the ranks. Captured *fedayin* whom I have seen have resembled the lowest type of criminal. These men did great damage and murdered right and left. Often they would lie hidden behind innocent-looking cactus hedges or in orange groves. My driver taught me always to have a pistol handy. 'Either he shoots first, or you do.'

The Israelis fought back, and several times shocked the world by the ruthlessness of their retaliations. This would be the pattern of such an operation. The intelligence would locate the position of a *fedayin* hide-out and plans would be laid. One dark night army units would go out, capture the position, kill all the men, and destroy the buildings.

As time passed it became increasingly apparent that some violent explosion could be expected. It was sparked off in October 1956 when Jordan joined the Egyptian-Syrian pact. The iron ring surrounding Israel was now complete and the economic blockade had been turned into a military siege. On almost the same day the Israeli intelligence service reported that 2500 new *fedayin* had been trained, and that it was expected they would be stationed on the Israeli borders. In a coordinated operation they would invade Israel and strike terror into her people. Their morale destroyed, the combined army would march in and administer the final blow.

Israel's reply to the challenge was immediate. On Monday October 29th, at 4.30 p.m. Ben-Gurion took the fatal decision. In the event of war most people had assumed that it would be against Jordan; but instead the Israeli army crossed the frontier into Sinai. The target was Egypt.

A nation of 2,000,000 had challenged one of 24,000,000, and moreover one that had been armed to the teeth, by the Eastern bloc. The last point is important. Nasser's arms pact with Moscow in 1955 had meant that the balance of power had shifted significantly against Israel. Egypt had quickly obtained formidable supplies of modern weapons, Mig fighters and Ilyushin bombers, fast and heavy tanks of Stalin III and T-34 types, heavy guns, and equipment of all kinds. Israel, on the other hand, was isolated. Military material these days soon becomes obsolete, and the arms which had helped her to win in 1948 and 1956 were now not much more than scrap. She had appealed to the Western Powers in vain; the West, anxious to avoid giving offence to the Arab oil-producing countries, had turned a deaf ear to all her requests, except that at the last moment France had agreed to fill gaps in her defence by providing large supplies chiefly of Mystère fighters. Paris had realized that Israel was the only Mediterranean Power on which she could rely in her stand against the Algerian rebels. It is typical of Ben-Gurion that he prefaced this encouraging news in announcing it to the Knesset by quoting a long poem by Nathan Altermann about the fateful night when the scales were tipped.

In the event the campaign proved to be one of the shortest in the whole history of war. Two days after the attack had been launched the Egyptian army was in full retreat through the desert. In less than 100 hours the Israeli army had reached the Suez Canal, had captured the whole of Sinai, and had raised the blockade of the Gulf of Aqaba; Gaza, now completely isolated, fell like a ripe plum into Israeli hands. How is such an incredible result to be explained? Captain Liddell Hart, the British authority on modern warfare, has called the Sinai campaign 'a masterpiece of strategic art'. Israeli material was greatly inferior to that of Egypt, but the Israeli leadership outmanœuvred the Egyptian in its keen appreciation of 'the dual principles of speed and surprise that are fundamental to success in war'. And Liddell Hart goes on: 'Israel has developed an army which in quality stands on the top level. Indeed, on the evidence of its performance, I think it would be hard to match as a combination of determination, mobility, and flexibility.' The Napoleonic maxim that in war the psychological is to the physical as three is to one had been confirmed yet again.

At the same time it would be wrong to infer that the Egyptian troops are poor fighting material; the ordinary Egyptian soldier is both brave and tough. The Israelis, however, struck repeatedly where they were least expected; and in far too many cases the Egyptian officers were inferior, all too ready to give up, and even to abandon their men. In such a situation it is not surprising that many of the men dropped their weapons, and pulling off their boots fled across the desert. There are some revealing figures. In the last Israeli reprisal action before the Sinai war the battalions in action had nineteen killed, of whom seventeen were officers. But of the 5000–6000 Egyptians captured in Sinai, only 200 were officers. When the town of El Arish in Sinai was taken, an Israeli army doctor inspecting the field hospital found no officers, no doctors, and no nurses; they had all fled. The only person in the operating theatre was one of the wounded, and he lay dead under an anaesthetic, abandoned to his fate.

The Israeli army is led by young officers. 'Our generals are boys, that's why we win our wars,' I have often heard it said. Yigal Yadin was thirty-one when he won the war of 1948. The commanding officer in Sinai, Moshe Dayan, the man with the familiar black eyeshade, was forty-one. During the campaign Dayan inspected a unit which lay inactive in front of the Egyptian position, and gave its commander an hour in which to capture it. As he had failed to do so by then he dismissed him on the spot and appointed a new one, who succeeded in taking the position. 'The nearest way to victory is the one which leads to the enemy position,' was one of Dayan's maxims. An amusing story is told in Tel Aviv about a young soldier who had returned home from Sinai. He spoke in enthusiastic terms of the campaign, referring repeatedly to the youth of the officers. Wishing to restrain the young man's ardour, his father remarked that at any rate Ben-Gurion, the man ultimately responsible for the victory, was past seventy. Whereupon the young man exclaimed: 'Ah yes, of course Ben-Gurion is twice thirty-five!'

Many stories are told of individual exploits which helped to win the campaign. One of these concerns the parachutists who were dropped at the start near the Suez Canal, with the object of cutting the strategic road through the Mitla Pass. Holding out against air and land attacks for three or four days until the arrival of the main force, they suffered heavy losses. There is also the story of the Egyptian destroyer *Ibrahim el Awar*, which caused much amusement when it surrendered to an Israeli aeroplane during an attack on Haifa. It is extremely rare for a warship to surrender at all, and only one did so in the Second World War. The *Ibrahim el Awar*, as HMS *Cottesmore*, had taken part in the Normandy landings and had been sold to Egypt after the war. British naval officers called it 'The ship which died of shame.'

Operation Kadesh was the Israeli code name for the campaign. The name is taken from the Bible; Kadesh Barnea is the place where Moses made the people of Israel spend a long time in the desert. As they marched through Sinai the troops were also reminded of Abraham and Isaac, who had been there even earlier. The reverberation of gunfire had hardly died away before a scientific expedition had set out from Jerusalem to explore the peninsula; it included archaeologists, historians, philologists, geographers, botanists, and zoologists.

The site of the historical Mountains of Sinai is unknown. Traditionally it is Jebel Musa (which is Arabic for 'Mountains of Moses'), a granite mass, 6000–10,000 feet high, in southern Sinai. Near it is the ancient Greek Orthodox monastic church of St Catherine, which the scientists used as their headquarters, and which possesses an extremely interesting library. The monastery was built in A.D. 330; the library contains books and scrolls in many languages, besides 3200 old manuscripts. Its greatest treasure is no longer there. This is the Codex Sinaiticus, the Greek translation of the Old Testament which was found in the library just over 100 years ago. The discovery caused as great a sensation among scholars then as the recent discovery and deciphering of the Dead Sea scrolls. The Codex Sinaiticus was borrowed by the Czar of Russia, who 'forgot' to return it, and instead sold it to the British Museum.

One day young Israeli troops climbed to the top of the Jebel

Musa and on the spot where the Lord traditionally spoke to Moses and gave him the tablets of the Commandments raised the Israeli flag.

Moses spent many years in Sinai, but his descendants were not allowed to remain there for more than a few months. The United Nations, by an overwhelming majority of the General Assembly, branded Israel as an aggressor. But, as Mr Selwyn Lloyd, the British Foreign Secretary at the time, said: 'If a man threatens to cut your throat and you kick the knife out of his hand—are you an aggressor?'

Israel evacuated Sinai. But before taking the narrative any further, let us consider one or two small points which are not without significance. An Israeli foundation in Jerusalem, called Keren Hayesod, publishes an annual calendar giving Biblical quotations for each month. It seems almost as though by intention that for the month which corresponds to November 1956 there is the quotation:

'In that day it shall be said to Jerusalem, Fear thou not: and to Zion, Let not thine hands be slack.'

The motto for December was from Jeremiah:

'And I will make thee unto this people a fenced brazen wall: and they shall fight against thee, but they shall not prevail against thee: for I am with thee to save thee and to deliver thee, saith the Lord.'

The January text is from Leviticus:

'And I will give peace in the land, and ye shall lie down, and none shall make you afraid.'

The Israeli campaign against Egypt coincided with the Hungarian revolution. During those days the world experienced one of the most dangerous crises since the defeat of Germany. And the situation was to get worse. On the day after Israeli troops had crossed the border a comparatively local affair was magnified into world dimensions when Britain and France issued an ultimatum to the belligerents calling for a withdrawal from the Suez Canal. A few months earlier Nasser had announced the nationalization of the canal and from then on the dictator had his finger on the main artery between Western Europe and the Middle East, able to tighten his grip and stop the flow of traffic whenever it suited him. Given the will and the ability in the summer of 1956 France and Britain might have occupied the canal without serious risk; the world was so affronted by Nasser's action that hardly anyone would have protested. But the required troops were not available and so instead they negotiated; then after a good deal of arguing and intriguing, the whole matter was turned over to the United Nations. Nevertheless behind the scenes British and French staff officers drew up the plans of Operation Terrapin (Tortoise) aimed at the canal.

There have been prolonged arguments as to whether there was collusion between the two Powers and Israel, an agreement to the effect that Britain and Israel would strike when Israel had attacked. It has been alleged that Ben-Gurion secretly visited Paris to make the final preparations with Guy Mollet, the French Prime Minister. Of course all the rumours and reports were denied, and of course nobody believed the denials. Anyone who tries to ferret out the facts now meets with silence all round. 'No one has succeeded in raising a corner of the veil of secrecy which surrounds Sinai and Suez,' I was told by the Prime Minister's office in Jerusalem, 'and it will be a long time before anyone does.'

Still, certain facts stand out. For example, as early as October 29th the French Air Force stationed large units of Mystère fighters in Israel. These never went into action, but were held in reserve in order to protect the open towns of Israel against raids by superior Egyptian forces. Israel and France must have laid down certain lines of common strategy before the war developed. Relations between Jerusalem and London, however, had for some years been cool, so that in this case it is difficult to think that any collusion could have been possible. The commander of the Allied expeditionary force, General Sir Charles

Keightley, when asked by one of his officers in Cyprus what were his instructions in the event of his making contact with Israeli troops, replied with a quick gesture descriptive of the wringing of a chicken's neck. Moshe Dayan was interviewed on the same subject in Tel Aviv. It should be stated here that when the British in 1941 were planning to invade Syria from Palestine in order to prevent the Germans from occupying it, they asked for Palestine Jews as guides. Dayan was in a British prison for illegal activities, but was freed and led the advance column into Syria, losing an eye in the operation. Reminding him of this exploit, the journalist remarked:

'You collaborated with the British then.'

Dayan replied: 'It was the Australians.'

Operation Terrapin took its slow course, in speed the direct opposite of Israel's own war against Egypt. Though the air raids may have helped to soften up the Egyptians, they took far too long. Nasser, on the verge of collapse, was allowed time in which to recover. Once more then the cat landed on all fours. Port Said had been occupied and the southward advance had begun along the Suez Canal when it was suddenly halted. Britain was split on the issue and there were dramatic scenes in the House of Commons. The United States, at odds with her allies, threatened to block British credits, a step which would have caused a fall of the pound. Russia threatened nuclear attack unless the action was called off. Sir Anthony Eden, sick and hard pressed, gave way and Port Said was evacuated. Once more Israel was isolated. Under personal pressure from President Eisenhower, Ben-Gurion and the Knesset agreed to evacuate Sinai and Gaza.

The Franco-British attack was a bloomer; by the time it started the issue had been decided. Israel had already won. The victory in Sinai, if allowed to develop, would have brought about the downfall of the Nasser régime. Now Nasser was able to cover up his defeat in Sinai by concentrating his propaganda campaign on the two major Powers; Cairo radio proclaimed him as the victor.

Nevertheless the war was not fought in vain. United Nations

troops stationed at Sharm el Sheikh have succeeded in preserving peace in these sensitive border areas. What is more, the action of the Israeli army revealed that Russia, under cover of the arms pact with Nasser, had established a base in Sinai. The Russian arms dumps there were on a scale and of a type that the Egyptian army could never have used.

It was the tip of the Russian arrow which pointed south to the oil of the Middle East. This was to be more clearly apparent in the years to come. We will now turn to Iraq.

During the middle of the night a telephone rang in a bedroom in Washington. Mr Allan Dulles, head of the American intelligence service, suddenly sat up when he heard the news:

'Revolution in Baghdad; the royal family murdered.'

The news had caught all America napping. That same day the President of the Lebanon, M. Camille Chamoun, asked for United States help against the revolution which threatened his pro-Western government, and this time America was ready; a few hours later Bikini girls and their boy friends basking on the beach at Beirut saw the 'grey diplomats' appear on the horizon. Landing craft of the sixth American fleet made for the coast and the 'Leathernecks', the United States marines, waded ashore. Two days later King Hussein of Jordan asked for British aid; and the 'Red Devils' were flown in to Amman from Cyprus. Western intervention in the Middle East was in full swing.

The explosion in Baghdad took place on the night of July 14, 1958. The ageing Prime Minister, Nuri es Said, had been uneasy. Fourteen times he had held office, and though he had fallen many times he had always managed to work his way back into power. A loyal ally of the West, he had forced his people to follow the same course. But times were bad and the propaganda from Cairo was having its effect; the people were boiling over. A few months before, Nasser had gained a victory when the union with Syria had been proclaimed, and during the last two weeks he had held out a hand to both the Lebanon and Jordan. Trouble flared up in the Lebanon; in Jordan King Hussein's throne tottered under the blasts of Egyptian propaganda. A day or two before the fateful night Nuri had given telephonic orders for the third division of the Iraqi army, then stationed at Basra on the Persian Gulf, to advance swiftly towards Amman and be ready for intervention. The divisional commander, Abdel Karim el-Kassem, aged forty-four, was a man who could keep his own counsel. When Nuri replaced the receiver he could not have known that he had just signed his own death warrant. For years Kassem had been planning to overthrow Nuri and the royal house, and now the moment had arrived. In order to get to Amman the division had to pass through Baghdad. It was now or perhaps never.

On the night of July 14th, then, the long columns marched into the slumbering city on the banks of the Tigris. Quietly the bridges and the Ministries and radio station were occupied; then the command was given to advance on the palace. The new rulers have never revealed the details of the coup, but the twenty-three-year-old King Faisal was murdered, as were the Queen Mother, the King's sister, and his uncle, the forty-four-year-old 'Crown Prince' Abdulillah, one of the régime's best hated men, whose body was dragged naked through the city behind a jeep. By now the mob was up and had filled the streets. It was given free hands; and it murdered and slashed, and stormed and set fire to British and American offices. Eventually, at three in the afternoon, the authorities imposed a curfew.

The biggest prize, however, had escaped; Nuri es Said had got away. A fox has more than one exit from its earth, and Nuri had long since had a secret tunnel dug from his bedroom. Escaping through this, he had found a temporary refuge in a brothel, whose proprietress had for years been a friend of his. But she dared not keep him for more than a day or two; and so, disguised as a woman, he tried to slip out. Unfortunately for him, the women of Baghdad are small and he was tall and powerful. A boy in the street noticed his pyjama trousers protruding from his dress and began to whistle and shout; a few minutes later Nuri was dead. A photograph of his mutilated body in the street, which came out of Iraq, is so gruesome that the British Press shrank from printing it.

This macabre drama has its ironical side. The sole heir to the immense fortune in dollars of the murdered Prime Minister was a young Israeli boy. This is the strange story which lies behind the will. In 1939 Nuri's son, Sabach, fell in love with a pretty young Jewess, by name Nadja. The two families lived in the same street, where their palaces stood side by side. Both fathers were opposed to the match. The Prime Minister was against his only son marrying a Jewess; and like a true Jew Nadja's father did not want her to marry a non-Jew. In the end the two young people married secretly; and when, the following year, Nadja gave birth to a son, Nuri became reconciled to them. The boy, however, led to the break-up of the marriage; for Sabach wanted to bring him up as a Moslem, and Nadja had him circumcized, on the eighth day according to the Law of Moses, and admitted to the covenant of Abraham. The father was furious and obtained a divorce. Nadja managed to escape to Tel Aviv before the coup, with £1000 in sterling which she had received from her father-in-law. She invested the money well and now owns a fashionable hotel. Meanwhile, Sabach married again, and by his new wife, a Moslem, had two more sons. But parents and children were among the murdered when the mob forced the royal palace, their bodies being thrown into the Tigris. Of course the grandson in Tel Aviv received none of the fortune in Baghdad; but like every other prominent Arab Nuri had prepared for a possible exile and invested a million dollars in Swiss and British banks. The fate of this fortune is subject to international law and falls to the boy in Israel.

At first, everyone thought that Nasser was behind the revolt in Iraq, but for once the Egyptian conspirator was as surprised as was Mr Allan Dulles. Moreover, Kassem soon showed that he had no intention to behave like a disciplined follower of Nasser but had a policy of his own. This austere officer, who is for an Arab statesman remarkably silent and reserved, is a man

Ain Karen, near Jerusalem

Damming of the winter rainfall in the Negev

Working in a kibbutz

New houses at Ashdod

The road to the Dead Sea

of mystery. But the world soon learnt the answers to some of the problems he represented. It became clear that Britain had lost one of her most loyal allies among the Arab nations, and the Baghdad pact the member whose capital had given to it its name. Yet instead of breaking off every tie with Britain, Kassem seeks to pursue a middle course and hold open the doors to both East and West. Iraq is the only Arab country which gets arms from both; and to everyone's surprise Kassem has refrained, so far at any rate, from taking over the Western-run oil companies.

The régime enjoys the full support of the army and Kassem is safe for as long as he can hold it. Consequently, he keeps the army under close observation and is continually purging its corps of officers. He believes in a small but loyal army rather than a big one which might one day knock on his door as he once knocked on the King's. Nevertheless there are pressures from both sides, and both Nasserites and Communists are contending for the prize of Iraq.

For long Nasser hoped to win Iraq, and were he to succeed he would become, with the riches of the Iraq oilfields at his command, the undisputed lord of the Arabs. He tried by fair means, and when these failed he tried foul ones. Not content with the usual intriguing, he provoked a rebellion in the oil centre of Mosul, sent his legionaries across the frontier from Syria, and caused assassins to lie in wait for Kassem. More than once they have nearly succeeded; and Cairo radio clamours ceaselessly for Kassem's death.

Baghdad is another great objective of Russian expansion; and under persistent pressure from Nasser, Kassem was forced to lean on the Communists. He now has Communists on his staff, in key Ministerial posts, and in high places in the army. As always the Kremlin is clever and insidious; it does not seek rapid results but is actively consolidating its positions. Not a Communist revolution, but an evolution towards Communism is its aim.

One wonders what will happen if Kassem should suddenly die; perhaps at the hand of one of Nasser's hirelings. As far as

Israel is concerned, there would be no change. Kassem calls for her destruction; and whoever the successor, he would do the same.

Our survey of Israel's neighbours is nearly concluded. The Lebanon border on the north is quiet, and if the Lebanon dared she would make peace with her neighbour. There remains Syria, the neighbour across the Lake of Gennesaret and the northern reaches of the Jordan. Here is another frontier of barbed wire and hatred and sudden clashes. Syria was for long a political vacuum, where one revolution followed another in rapid succession. The Russians saw their chances and infiltrated farther than they had been able to do in any other Arab country. Then Nasser struck and Syria became a province of the United Arab Republic.

Syria consented because she had no choice, but the alliance was never popular. The Syrians are a proud nation and they saw themselves being ruled by a man out of Africa, and therefore, to them, a black man. They also found the experiment a costly one; Egypt derived all the economic benefits from the union, while Syria paid the bill. Here are a few examples. Syria was an exporter of cotton, but Egypt had a surplus of cotton too and forced her partner to restrict her production. The same happened in the textile industry, where again Syrian standards were high. Syrian factories began to close down, while Nasser opened new ones in Egypt. For the first time in her history Syria was obliged to import wheat. The Egyptian land reforms, providing for the breaking up of estates, was extended to Syria. The response of the owners was to leave their fields uncultivated, with the result that there was a fall in wheat production.

Syria was disaffected, and the dissatisfaction grew daily more bitter. In the autumn of 1961 she struck and recovered her independence. Her future still hangs in the balance.

News of the bloodbath in Baghdad was read in the airport at Zürich by a Jewish couple who were on their way from Johannesburg to visit relatives in Tel Aviv. They immediately despatched a telegram:

'Journey cancelled due disturbances.'

A few hours later they received the reply:

'Sorry disturbances there. Come here.'

The telegram is typical of Israeli coolness in a crisis. Like a small island in the midst of a sea which could inundate it at any moment it remains confident of survival. One reason for Israel's confidence is the disunity and self-destructive policies of her neighbours, as the foregoing pages will have shown. There is an amusing story which illustrates this.

A scorpion wished to cross the Nile, and so it asked permission to sit on a camel's back when it swam across. The camel, however, was suspicious.

'Can I be sure you won't sting me once we're out in the middle?' it asked.

'Why should I sting you?' asked the scorpion. 'If I sting you you'll drown, and I'll drown with you.'

This sounded very reasonable, and so the camel allowed the scorpion to climb on to its back. It soon realized, however, that it had made a mistake, for no sooner were they in midstream than it received a mortal sting. As it sank it turned its head in the direction of the scorpion, and said:

'Why on earth did you do that? Now we shall both die.'

'My friend,' replied the scorpion, 'this is the Middle East.'

VI

PERSONS AND POLITICS

꠸

CHAIM WEIZMANN was in the United States at the time of his election as the first President of the new Israel. Before leaving to take over his high office he had talks with President Truman, in the course of which it is reported that the following exchange took place. Mr Truman observed:

'I am president of 150 million Americans, and you of a million and a half Israelis.'

'You are wrong,' Weizmann replied, 'I am the president of a million and a half presidents.'

The remark makes a significant point. Jews are individualists in all things, including politics, and it has been said that where three Jews are gathered together there will be four political parties. Twenty-one parties contested the first General Election to the Knesset, and nine won seats. The number has not grown fewer with the years. At the election in November 1959 there were twenty-four parties and 1291 candidates contesting 120 seats. Ten got represented.

In this respect Israel resembles France during the Fourth Republic; there is the same array of parties, the same perpetual political crises and prolonged discussions before a government can be formed.

Other countries, such as Britain and America, have settled for the two-party system, and there are people in Israel who advocate the abandonment of the present system of proportional representation and the introduction of elections by constituency, which by eliminating many small parties would make for greater stability. This reform is in Ben-Gurion's programme, but there is little prospect of its adoption. Nor could Israel, at present, make do with fewer than three parties; besides Conservatives and Social Democrats (Labour), there would have to be a religious group. Moreover, it is a widely held belief that every shade of opinion ought to be represented, even the most eccentric. Just as in modern law it is considered better that a hundred guilty men should go free than that one innocent man should be condemned, so in Israel it is thought better to submit to a hundred tons of nonsense than to suppress a grain of intelligence.

The same tangled scene meets the eye of the observer who stops at a news-stand in Tel Aviv or Jerusalem. In this small nation of a little over 2,000,000 there are twenty-three newspapers. The proliferation of papers is due, of course, to the fact that the nation is in the melting-pot, made up, as it is, of immigrants from a wide range of countries. They all want papers in their own languages; and as a result there are dailies or weeklies not only in Hebrew and Yiddish, but also in Arabic, English, German, French, Polish, Russian, Rumanian, Bulgarian, Italian, Hungarian. Most of them are politically coloured, many of them very definitely so. To every party its paper in every language, seems to be the aim. This is in striking contrast to the West, where the trend is towards a progressive concentration in a few mass-circulation papers.

Lack of political interest is a frequent complaint in the West, but in Israel the interest in politics is so great that it occasionally becomes fanatical. Keen political arguments are common in the *kibbutzim* and have sometimes led to a split, so that the minority has left. Important issues can give rise to violent demonstrations, and minor ones may lead to Government crises.

The violent contrasts are not new to Israel but were inherited from its parent Zionism, which was always at issue with itself. There must be few historical movements which have been shaken by so many convulsions. The leaders have always been strong personalities; and all too often they have been unable to agree among themselves; not, of course, as to their final aims, but on the means. One of the major disagreements was that between the two greatest Zionists after Herzl—Chaim Weizmann and David Ben-Gurion.

When he became Israel's President Weizmann was a man of seventy-four with a long life of work behind him. Like many of the best men of his country he came from Russia, where he was born in 1874, at a village near Pinsk, in the area of Jewish settlement. Herzl had been a typical assimilated Jew, who had to work a long passage home. Weizmann, on the other hand, was born in the midst of a vital Jewish community. He attended the Orthodox *heder* as a boy, and went on a *yeshiva*. The pogroms and exclusion from the university drove this gifted young man first to Berlin and then to Switzerland. Eventually he arrived in England, where he became a reader in biochemistry at Manchester University.

Tactful and reserved, he took naturally to the British way of life from the start; as a realist, shunning phrase-making and big talk, inclining to under-statement, he became to the English an Englishman. In the First World War the Jews were divided, some on either side. By this time the leadership of the British branch of Zionism was in Weizmann's hands, and he acquired wide influence in the international leadership. During these years he was brought into contact with leading British statesmen, engaged at the time in planning the post-war world. David Lloyd George was a man with roots in the Bible, and Weizmann struck an answering chord in him. The same is true of his relations with Balfour, and a conversation between these two has become historical and is typical of the Zionist perspective. Britain had offered the Zionists the colonization of Kenya, which then formed a part of British Uganda, as a compensation for Palestine. Herzl had accepted the proposal, but had been bitterly opposed by Weizmann and the majority of Zionists. Balfour had been surprised by Weizmann's dislike of the idea and had tried to win him over to it. When Balfour had finished speaking, Weizmann suddenly asked:

'How would you like to have Paris as your capital instead of London?'

'I wouldn't, but then we have London,' Balfour replied in astonishment.

'True,' Weizmann said, 'and we had Jerusalem when London was a swamp.'

Balfour never forgot this reply.

Weizmann, a brilliant chemist, rendered valuable services to Britain. In 1915 he discovered a new method of making high explosives, and he also worked on the production of synthetic rubber. Both were vital to the war effort. But his greatest achievement was his influence on British statesmen which led to the Balfour Declaration.

Level-headed realist as he was, Weizmann realized that the issue could not be settled by a declaration alone, no matter how far-reaching. That could be no more than a framework, which the Jewish people would have to fill out themselves.

Accordingly, Weizmann always supported any endeavour which would tend to relate ancient Hebrew tradition with modern knowledge. The college and the Hebrew University which he founded when Allenby's guns were still hammering the Turks in Palestine were among his favourite ambitions. He realized other ideas in the Weizmann Institute which he founded at Rehovat, where he also made his home. The three-fold foundation of Weizmann's 'synthetic Zionism' consists of politics, science, and colonization. The first two serve the last and furnish the conditions which will make the old country a new one. Moreover, it is in the village that the nation's soul resides. He knew from childhood that national values— language, literature, legends, and traditions—spring from man's intimate contact with the soil. 'I have seen swamps in the Valley of Jesreel drained and gradually become firm enough for red-roofed houses to be built on them. On dark nights the lights shone from them like beacons on our long journey home.'

In the history of Zionism, Weizmann is the outsider, as he is the solitary. He never became a man of the people, or a man whom the people took wholly to their hearts. By nature he was too distinguished and aristocratic for that, too much a friend of British statesmen, the guest of kings and presidents, aloof and a little chill in his manner. His discoveries brought him great wealth; socially and politically he stood well to the right of most Zionists. He also moved too slowly for most, yielded when he encountered obstacles, and spoke of moderation and caution when others sounded battle-cries. He believed in gradualness. Ben-Gurion practically said that if the heavens were to fall on Palestine Weizmann would urge moderation. As a result, he gradually receded and as President became chiefly a representative figure, increasingly divorced from political influence by the nature of his office. When Ben-Gurion gained control it was more than a change of generations which took place. Turbulent times called for a robuster man at the helm.

Without Weizmann, however, Israel would never have been established; and the words with which he summed up his life deserve to be remembered:

'Whether prophets will once more arise among the Jews in the near future it is difficult to say. But if they choose the way of honest and hard and clean living, on the land in settlements built on the old principles, and in cities cleansed of the dross which has sometimes been mistaken for civilization; if they centre their activities on genuine values, whether in industry, agriculture, science, literature, or art; then God will look down benignly on His children who after a long wandering have come home to serve Him with a psalm on their lips and a spade in their hands, reviving their old country and making it a centre of human civilization.'

Today Theodor Herzl and Chaim Weizmann stand as the two first great men of Zionism, men who have already become legendary. It was Herzl who saw the vision and Weizmann who began to realize it. But the results were not achieved without conflicts, especially when Herzl would have sacrificed Palestine for Kenya. Weizmann's attitude to Herzl was compounded of the pupil's admiration for his master and the criticism by the younger generation of its elders. The attitude of Ben-Gurion to Weizmann was the same; once again the young man built on the older man's foundations but also opposed and replaced him. Weizmann prevailed against Herzl. Ben-Gurion was born to prevail against Weizmann, and in his triumph convert Herzl's vision and Weizmann's practical achievement into the reality of everyday life.

David Ben-Gurion, too, was a native of Czarist Russia, but of that part of the Empire which had been Polish and would revert to Poland. He was born, in 1886, at Plonsk, forty-five miles to the north-west of Warsaw. His father was a lawyer; the home was well-to-do and a focus of local Zionist activities. The boy David Grün, as he was then called (he changed his name to the Hebrew form in Palestine), would sit in a corner of the room listening as his father talked to Zionist friends and received reports of conferences and resolutions and was told about pioneers in the distant land of their fathers. He also heard them talk of pogroms and of the Government's brutal treatment of the country's 6,000,000 Jews. Like many another young Jew in Russia and Poland he became a Socialist and a revolutionary. His father gave him the best possible secondary education and sent him to Warsaw in order to study law at the university. But David Grün's dreams were of Palestine, and one day the law student had become an agricultural labourer in an orange grove near Jaffa.

From that point his path was marked out. He arrived as a Socialist and he has always remained one. Active in the Labour movement from the start, he rose step by step to the highest positions in the land. David Ben-Gurion was of the people; and unlike Weizmann he has remained one of the people. He would appear to have been born under a lucky star, for it is not often that one finds such inward and outward harmony as

in the life of Ben-Gurion. His personality provides an example
of a career which can begin in the trade unions and political
Labour movement and lead beyond narrow party limits to a
position representative of the nation, honoured and looked up
to by all. He was to be the leader whom the Jewish people
needed in their great hour of destiny, appearing from the heart
of the people at the crucial moment.

David Ben-Gurion differs from many competent politicians
in the richness and variety of his mind. In him, we find the
rare combination of wise man and realist: a Biblical prophet in
the figure of a modern statesman. It is no secret that in the
critical days at the beginning of May 1948 most of his
colleagues had grave doubts. The Foreign Minister designate,
Moshe Shertok, advised against the proclamation and instead
recommended a policy of wait and see. Many were of the same
opinion. But Ben-Gurion was convinced that it was now or
never. Had he not seen his vision and in the end converted his friends, all would now have been different. If
there is one man to whom the credit is due for taking
the right turn at the cross-roads, that man is Ben-Gurion.
He seized an opportunity at a point of time when all was
ripe, and the result was the Jewish State. It is the ability to
see beyond the immediate tangle of events which makes a
statesman of a politician.

Ben-Gurion makes a vivid impression on all who meet him.
He is thickset and stocky and his head seems strangely large
for his body. That is what leads one to think of him as taller
than he really is. He has a pronounced profile and shrewd and
animated eyes which have a smile in their corners. The first
thing which attracts the attention, however, is his large head
of white hair above a bald crown, reminding one rather of a
lion's mane. Stories are told about this hair. Some friends were
talking together about the poor state of the Israeli economy, and
one of them remarked:

'Everything's black in Israel; the market and everything
else.'

To which one of the others replied:

'If things hadn't been so black, Ben-Gurion's hair wouldn't have been so white.'

In the course of a long life Ben-Gurion has borne the burdens of his people and he has clearly aged in the process. He has had to pay the price of a man who makes history. Of course he has his faults; without contrasts and cleavages he would not be a Jew. And his origins in Russia, where the Jews had to resort to devious means against a corrupt administration, have left their influence on him. His opponents fear him as a political tactician, knowing that in the labyrinths of party politics he does not shrink from tough and at times doubtful methods. A strong man, he is often suspected of dictatorial leanings. It is not that he aspires to be an autocrat; he knows history and the faults of dictators far too well for that. But it is true that his forceful character has too often dominated other members of the Government, sometimes forcing them into accepting more extreme policies than their consciences approve of. Jewish wit is quick to pounce on such things and impale him on its shafts, as in this story:

'Why doesn't Ben-Gurion get himself proclaimed as King of Israel?'

'Because he wouldn't like to be David the Second.'

This man of strength and defects, with the highlights and shadows richly faceted in his character, should not be seen only in the light of political clashes, wars, and other great events. We cannot properly understand him until we realize that he is a Jew. He feels himself deeply rooted in Jewish thought and tradition, at one and the same time indebted to and limited by Judaism in all its glories and triumphs as well as its bitter tragedies. The Jewish feeling is perhaps most strongly marked when Ben-Gurion speaks. He is a great speaker, one who loves words, loves to read, talk, and listen, has sharpened his wits and his style in countless debates and arguments. He first made an impact on the public from the platform, and it was there that he developed his ideas to the pitch where they became memorable and inspiring. Like Sir Winston Churchill he has the gift of epigrammatic utterance. At the outbreak of the

Second World War, soon after the publication of the British White Paper which the Jews considered a betrayal, Ben-Gurion proclaimed the celebrated slogan:

'We will fight on Britain's side as if there were no White Paper; and we will fight the White Paper as if there were no war.'

In his highest flights of oratory it is the Jew who speaks. The language is permeated with the thoughts and style of the Bible; on occasion, indeed, he has quoted whole chapters from the Law and the Prophets which fitted in to the context of his speech. He has a deep grasp of the Bible, which is his chief source of inspiration; he draws strength for his personality and for his work from that and from Jewish history.

Ben-Gurion has always been a controversial figure. He has always spoken his mind, even when what he had to say was unpopular, and he has pursued his aims with pertinacity, especially in the two causes nearest to his heart: the repatriation of the exiles and the conquest of the desert. As Ben-Gurion sees it, a Zionist is not a man who pays somebody to settle in Palestine, but one who goes home to Zion himself. And although 1,000,000 have done so since the State was established, he regards this as only a beginning. He has spoken so sharply of Jews who, while contributing large sums of money to Israel, themselves prefer the fleshpots of Egypt, that there was once a risk of a breach between him and American Jews. They, of course, were the ones he had in mind. And it is a fact that the desert will have to be conquered; for its dead emptiness is the country's major enemy. Once Palestine was a 'land flowing with milk and honey'. In centuries of neglect it degenerated, and the old fertility must be restored for the good of those millions whom Ben-Gurion expects to bring home. He has never asked anyone to do what he has not already done himself or is prepared to do. Thus he personally took the lead in the war against the desert when, in 1952, he resigned as Prime Minister and settled with his wife at Sde Boker, a new and primitive *kibbutz* in the middle of the Negev, where they lived for a year among young settlers.

One who showed the way: that was always Ben-Gurion. After the First World War he showed the way to the objective of a Jewish State. He was one of those who created the remarkable organization that was to be the seed from which the State would grow.

That organization was the Histadruth. The name is an abbreviation of the Hebrew word for Trades Union Centre—or TUC. The first settlers in Palestine had first to readjust themselves. For countless centuries the Jews had lived by one-sided urban occupations as merchants, bankers, artisans, doctors, lawyers. In Palestine they had to start afresh; the settler wanted to be a workman or a farmer. It is not easy to carry out such a revolution, and many wore themselves out before they learnt to hold their own against the British and the Arabs. Not only occupationally but socially and culturally as well they encountered problems. The trade-union movement which they established was therefore so widely based that it is without an equal.

The Histadruth is a federation of labour unions in agriculture, industry, building, transport, shops and offices, the postal services, and so on, with the object of protecting the workers' industrial and economic interests and improving wages and working conditions. In these respects the Histadruth is like any other trade-union organization. There, however, the resemblance ends. With increasing immigration it felt impelled to take on the tasks of social welfare, because no one else had done so. Members of the Histadruth pay a contribution, based on their income, which goes to provide social security. A large associated health organization, the Kupat Holim, is responsible for medical attention, hospital treatment, medicines, and so on. The Histadruth also cares for the aged, invalids, widows, and orphans. When the State was established, it became closely associated with the public authorities, and all forms of social service have been rapidly developed.

The Histadruth also has its cultural side. For a time it organized schools, classes, and training colleges, and it still provides teaching in Hebrew, trains teachers of choral singing and folk dancing, promotes amateur drama and study groups, runs a professional theatre, and publishes a daily newspaper. All co-operative societies belong to it, and most agricultural foods are distributed through its shops and restaurants. The country bus services are also a child of the Histadruth.

The most remarkable feature of this truly unique organization has yet to be named; for, besides representing the interests of the workers, the Histadruth took an early share in the country's industrial activities, so that it is today also the biggest employer in Israel. Among the undertakings which it controls is the Solel Boneh, which is one of the biggest building and contracting businesses in the Middle East, together with factories in a range of industries. It builds houses, and it owns its own banks for financing its other operations.

The headquarters of the Histadruth are a palatial building in Tel Aviv which popular wit has named the Kremlin. The building is an index of the vast organization which it accommodates, an organization whose influence is felt on all sides.

The 1948 war was over and the people of Israel returned to their daily activities. At the beginning of 1949 they went to the polls in order to elect their first Parliament, the Knesset. It was a 'khaki election', as many men and women were still in uniform, and the result was awaited with some excitement. Let us pause for a moment to consider the multiplicity of parties.

The Labour and Socialist movement was split, as it still is. The larger wing is known as the Mapai, a name formed from the Hebrew initials of the Israeli Labour Party. This is Ben-Gurion's party and it corresponds to the Labour parties of Britain and Scandinavia. The other wing is the Mapam, which means United Labour Party; this is a left-wing Labour party which sympathizes with Soviet Russia. The number of actual Communists is and has always been small; a large proportion are Arabs who merely vote Communist in order to demonstrate their opposition to Israel. On the other side are Conservatives, called General Zionists, a few small Liberal groups, and the Heruth, which means 'Freedom'. The last-named group is formed from the remains of the terrorist organizations and their sympathizers; it is chauvinistic and calls for an aggressive foreign policy. Finally, there is a bloc which embraces the various degrees of Orthodoxy, and which strongly asserts the religious principles of Judaism and seeks to get them legally enforced.

The Mapai emerged from the election in 1949 as the largest party, commanding more than a third of the poll. The other major parties shared the remaining seats almost equally. In coalition with the Mapam, the Mapai could have had an absolute and powerful majority, and the two together would have controlled the Histadruth. But the Mapam refused to join up with the Mapai. Called upon to form a Government, Ben-Gurion had to seek support among the anti-Labour parties. The strange result was that the Mapai Socialists and the Orthodox formed a government together. The religious groups, holding the balance of power, were not to be ignored. They took advantage of the situation and exacted payment for their support.

This first coalition, it is almost unnecessary to say, was a very loose one, and time and again it was shaken by crises and intrigues. Smilingly, Ben-Gurion called the leading Orthodox Minister, Rabbi Maimon—the two have a high regard for each other and like to discuss important problems together—the 'Minister of Resignations'. This was because whenever Ben-Gurion neglected to take full account of Orthodox views, Rabbi Maimon at once threatened to resign; on more than one occasion the Orthodox Ministers demonstratively left the Government and provoked a serious crisis. There were delicate problems, of vital importance to the Orthodox, such as Sabbath legislation, kosher or ritually slaughtered meat, national service by women, marriage and divorce, education, and the burning question of what is a Jew. But although the coalition between these two parties often creaked at the joints and the

Orthodox adopted an oppositional standpoint, they have during most of the lifetime of Israel, remarkably enough, been in office together. They have not been the only coalition parties. Ben-Gurion is an able tactician, who trims his sail to the winds and has mastered the fine art of inducing other parties to share in the responsibility of government; at times these have included the General Zionists, at others the Mapam or its associated groups, and nearly always the government has included Liberals. There are, however, two parties with which Ben-Gurion will have no dealings: the Heruth and the Communists.

To follow the devious paths of Israeli politics would involve us in too many details. Israel is a democracy in its early stages; and it is a Jewish democracy. At the same time it is interesting to note how events in the world at large have frequently cast lengthy shadows over Israeli political life. Two of these have originated in countries which have had a share in determining the Jewish destiny; namely Russia and Germany.

There are many invisible ties between Russia and her satellites on the one hand and Israel on the other. Many of the 3,000,000 Russian Jews, as well as the hundreds of thousands who still live in other Eastern Europe countries, have relatives in Israel—either children, grandchildren, or more distant relations—and between Jews family ties are close. In 1952 came the great treason trial in Prague, and out of fourteen accused, eleven were Jews. Thousands of people in Israel listened in to the broadcast proceedings; some of them knew the prisoners, some of them perhaps were related to them. What they heard made a profound impression on them. They realized that this was not the old anti-Semitism of the mob, but a well-planned design on Judaism and Israel. An endless stream of propaganda was being directed against Zionism, which was stigmatized as the sin of all sins. Later they heard of the liquidation of the Jewish intelligentsia in Russia and the charge against the Russian doctors.

In Israeli politics it was the Mapam which paid the costs. Its members are doctrinaire zealots who see everything in terms of

Golda Meir

Monastery of the Sacred Cross

The way to the monastery of the Sacred Cross

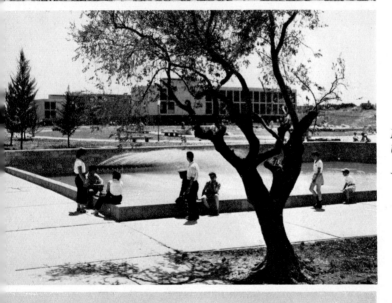

From the Hebrew University of Jerusalem

Faculties in the University centre

black and white; their opponents do not deny their idealism.
'When they talk they say an awful lot of nonsense; but when
they act they do wonderful things.' They founded *kibbutzim*
in unhealthy swamps; they formed a large proportion of the
Israeli shock troops, the *Palmach* units, during the war. They
have only one plank in their platform: collaboration with
Soviet Russia.

The pressure of events proved too strong for them, and the
party split into four parts. One part went Communist purely
and simply. The biggest group, calling itself Ahdut Avodah
(United Labour), has some outstanding leaders and is Socialist
in domestic affairs while in foreign affairs it is almost as
chauvinistic as the Heruth.

Germany's attitude had even deeper repercussions. In 1952
Dr Adenauer offered Israel negotiations on some form of
indemnity for Jewish losses in the 'final solution'. Money can
never make good loss of life and untold misery; any compensation could be no more than a token. At the same time the
$715,000,000 agreed upon was, to Israel, an immense sum of
money.

When the matter became public the Israeli nation was split
in two, and the gulf seemed unbridgeable. Hatred of everything
German had been so great that many of its manifestations were
grotesque. When it was discovered in Tel Aviv in 1949 that
the water mains were German, the contractor had to dig them
up and drop them in the sea.

In agreeing to open negotiations with Germany, Ben-Gurion
knew that he was risking his reputation and career, perhaps even
his life. There was great opposition and even his friends were
in two minds. The Heruth organized demonstrations which
developed into street fighting; the country seemed almost on the
verge of revolution.

Ben-Gurion, however, stood firm, believing that he was doing
the right thing. Now, of course, he has been proved right.
German goods come flowing in: industrial and agricultural
machinery, ships, locomotives, and much else. The agreement
has stimulated the Israeli economy. In 1959 there was a new

crisis when it was announced that Israel was supplying Germany with certain types of military equipment from a recently established arms factory. It was settled by Ben-Gurion's victory at the polls in November.

In the varied pattern of Israeli political life, Ben-Gurion stands out above all the rest. But he is surrounded by a number of men and women who are also outstanding.

Moshe Sharett, born in 1894, was only twelve years of age when his parents settled in Israel. Thus he grew up in the new country, and he was one of the first students of the new Herzlia grammar school at Tel Aviv. In the first eight years he was one of the most stable figures in Israeli political affairs, Foreign Minister throughout the period (a unique achievement in Israeli politics) and Prime Minister during the year when Ben-Gurion was at Sde Boker. It is due to Sharett that the diplomatic service was built up so quickly as it was.

Sharett is highly gifted and intelligent; a master of languages, witty and brilliant. The revival of Hebrew is a subject close to Sharett's heart; originally named Shertok, he adopted the Hebrew form Sharett, which is derived from 'Serve'. Possibly this indicates an awareness of his place, not as the principal leader, but a useful servant. All through life it has been his fate to stand in Ben-Gurion's shadow. They have been associated since before the First World War, though without ever becoming close friends; they are so different. Sharett is made of less robust material than Ben-Gurion. Where Ben-Gurion has original strength, gifted with breadth and depth as well as intuition, Sharett is the diplomat, a man of clear thought, calculation, and compromise. Ben-Gurion will grasp the kernel of a problem and act without a glance over his shoulder, whereas Sharett analyzes and dissects and studies the details before slowly reaching a conclusion. He could well be of the tribe of Reuben, of which Deborah sang in Judges: 'For the divisions of Reuben there were great searchings of heart.' It goes almost without saying that the two have often disagreed; indeed in 1956 they had a head-on clash. In the event Sharett resigned as

Minister of Foreign Affairs and retired from active political life, not without some bitterness. It is said that when Ben-Gurion, in tendering the party's thanks at a meeting after his resignation, referred to his thirty-seven years of service, Sharett rose to correct him:

'As usual the Prime Minister is wrong. It was thirty-eight years, not thirty-seven.'

During the period that he has been out of office, his abilities have been employed in many other directions, and he remains a great servant of his people.

Mrs Golda Meir succeeded Sharett as Foreign Minister when already a veteran of the Zionist movement. Born in 1898 at Kiev, 'the mother of Russian cities', she was driven from Russia with her family by the pogroms at the age of eight. They succeeded in reaching America, where her father worked as a joiner at Milwaukee, a city where 40,000 of the 500,000 inhabitants were Jews. Golda was a clever girl at school and was trained to be a teacher. So far there was nothing unusual in her career, but the turning-point came when she joined the Zionist Labour movement. A sister, nine years older than Golda, had married a young revolutionary in Russia. She was taken into their home, where she came into contact with both Zionism and Socialism, both of which influenced her for life. Travelling to Palestine, she settled in a *kibbutz*, where she went in for poultry farming. She might have gone on looking after poultry for the rest of her life, had she not been thrust into political affairs.

From then on her life was to be one of ceaseless activity. Golda Meir became a leader of women workers and attended congresses, and she was austere in her daily habits. In the struggle against the British Mandate she stood with Ben-Gurion, helped to organize illegal immigration, and at a critical time was political head of the Jewish Agency. After the proclamation of the State of Israel she went as Ambassador to Moscow, but was recalled to receive the appointment of Minister of Labour. Golda Meir has been a leading figure in the struggle for social security in Israel. As Foreign Minister she became for the first time a well-known international figure.

Mrs Golda Meir is a domestic figure also, who relaxes in her kitchen. While she is very feminine in her manner, her voice is strangely masculine, like an NCO's. The story goes that giving a blind beggar a coin one day, as she made a brief remark, she was greeted with the words: 'Thank you, sergeant.' Her strength lies in her balanced mind; Golda Meir is one of those people who are all of a piece.

Ben-Gurion is now well up in his seventies; and he hates old age. Looking out of the window one day and seeing an old man shuffle past, he exclaimed:

'Old age is a bad thing. Not an achievement but a defeat, something to be fought like other enemies.'

But the years go by and each lays its fresh burdens on the man. A burning question in Israel today is: Who will succeed Ben-Gurion? A strong man is like a big tree that smothers the lower growth around it. This is exemplified in the figure of Sir Winston Churchill, among others. But Ben-Gurion is alive to the problem, and at the election in 1959 brought forward the next generation. Three new men were then elected on the Mapai list. They were Abba Eban, the Israeli Ambassador to Washington and delegate to the United Nations; Moshe Dayan, the general of the Sinai campaign; and Simon Perez, head of the Foreign Ministry and the man who was associated with the French. The electoral success of the Mapai was due in large measure to these three men. But which is the 'Crown Prince', no one can say.

Chaim Weizmann died in 1952 and was succeeded as president by Isak Ben-Zwi. An amusing incident took place on the day of his installation. As the President and his wife were about to drive in state through the streets after the ceremony, it was found that their car had broken down. Instead of calling for another, Ben-Zwi took his wife by the arm and they walked to their unpretentious home amid cheers from the crowd.

Ben-Zwi and his wife are as simple and unpretentious in all their ways as this story suggests. The President was born in Russia and is a contemporary of Ben-Gurion: their careers have been closely identified and they have been friends and associates all their lives. If Ben-Zwi took second place, he is nevertheless a personality, and besides politics he has engaged in studies of Jewish folk life, especially in the Orient. The most famous Jew of our times, Albert Einstein, had been invited to become president, but declined. No doubt it was best that the man at the top should be one who had grown up with Zionism.

VII

FROM AFAR OFF

❦

'YOU see that boy at left half?'
The football match was in full swing, and the players were twelve-year-old boys. They streaked after the ball; one of them gained control, tried to dribble it past an opponent, and both fell. The head of the children's village was showing me round. We had been over dormitories, dining-rooms, common rooms, workshops, and had walked round the garden and watched boys and girls at work in the fields. We had finished up on the sports ground. The boy pointed out to me was thin and frail. As I looked he stopped, brushed his hair from his forehead, and kept an eye on the ball. Suddenly he dashed after it. But not before I had seen his face: his deep brow, narrow cheeks, and dark eyes. In the office the principal handed me a record of the boy's experiences, as he had been able to remember them. It was an incredible story.

His name was Ephraim and he came from Poland. He was under two years old when the Germans entered his home village in September 1939, and on the first day an SS man shot his mother. His father induced another woman to take charge of him, and a day or two later he also had been shot. The woman was afraid, for the penalty for hiding a Jew was death. She was tempted to get rid of him, even to kill him, but was afraid even of doing that, for had the body been found she would again have risked death. Another woman had been bayoneted for doing the same thing. Finally, she hid the boy in a drawer and under the bed. When visitors came to the house she would warn the boy by giving it a push. Thus Ephraim was still alive when Poland was occupied by the Red Army in 1944. But his only clothes were the tattered rags of his baby things, and he had been kept alive on what little the family had been able to spare from their own scanty rations. He had never learnt to walk. Found by his father's friend, he arrived, after many adventures, in Palestine. There, in the children's village, he had been restored to health. Now, at the age of twenty-two, he is studying medicine.

Children's villages exist in various parts of Israel. Originally intended for orphans like Ephraim, they are now more in the nature of general boarding schools. The children live together in groups according to their ages, and they receive instruction not only in general school subjects but also in practical ones, especially farming. Most of the children at these schools have come from far-off countries and have endured much.

This immigration goes under the special name of *Aliyah*, a Hebrew word which is used in the Book of Psalms of the ascent of the Hill of Zion to Jerusalem, 2500 feet high. In Jewish ears the word has an almost religious significance.

There have been Jews in Palestine since the days of Joshua, over 3000 years ago, and Jewish culture lived on there even after the dispersal. This Jewish population dwindled away at the time of the Crusades, but pockets remained here and there. There is, for example, a small village in the mountains of Galilee, called Peki'in, where, according to scholars such as Ben-Zwi, Jews have lived since Joshua's time. There have always been devout Jews who have come to die in Jerusalem.

The first Aliyah, however, came with the reawakening of national consciousness some eighty years ago and were called *Bilu* and *Hoveveh Zion*. They were less important for what they achieved as for the development which they started. Herzl had inspired the Jewish people; the Zionist movement took up the practical problems; and the Balfour Declaration provided a legal foundation for settlement in Palestine. But it was the violence in Europe during this century which gave impetus to this settlement, as one Aliyah followed another. The Russian pogroms, especially those which succeeded the unsuccessful revolution of 1905, the revolution of 1917 and the subsequent civil war, and above all the rise of Hitlerism were significant factors.

The great waves of immigrants before and after the First World War came from central and eastern Europe and were mostly made up of idealists. They usually settled in *kibbutzim* with the object of restoring the country's lost fertility. They were pioneers (*halutzim*), who drained the malaria-infested swamps, cleared desert scrub, and planted orange groves. They came because they felt the urge to come; for them Palestine was not a place of refuge, but *ha'aretz*, 'the country', the one to which all their thoughts aspired. They were followed by many who had been driven from a comfortable life in Germany and who turned to Palestine because they had nowhere else to go. In those years there was a rather malicious joke expressed in the question *'Kommen Sie aus Uberzeugung, oder kommen Sie aus Deutschland?'* ('Do you come from conviction, or from Germany?') For the majority the transplanting was a success; these German Jews were able to adjust themselves and they formed a valuable addition to the population. With the outbreak of the Second World War in 1939 immigration entered its most dramatic era. The recently published British White Paper had restricted the inflow to 1200 a month. It was like a drop in the ocean, and the consequent despair suggested other ideas. Illegal means seemed legal enough where the object was to save human lives.

This brings us to the fantastic story of *Aliyah Beth*. *Beth* is Hebrew for 'b'. Ordinary immigration was called *Aliyah Aleph*, or 'A immigration'. A relief organization all over Europe assisted refugees to make their way to Palestine. Of the 80,000 who got there in the war years 18,000 did so illegally. The world heard little about the ones who succeeded (for there was no reason to advertise their success) and more about the tragedies of those who failed.

For example, there was the steamship *Struma*, a former Rumanian cattle boat of 180 tons. A group of Jews succeeded in laying their hands on it and slipping out from a Rumanian port. There were 769 passengers on board this old vessel, including 200 women and children. The ship was in such a wretched condition that it was forced to seek refuge in Istanbul. The Jewish organization in Jerusalem did all they could to prevail upon the High Commissioner to grant visas for these refugees, but in vain. The captain therefore decided to make for Palestine illegally, and no more has ever been heard of the ship. Perhaps she struck a mine, perhaps was torpedoed, perhaps wrecked in a storm. The 769 passengers of course perished with her.

Other adventures ended more happily, including that of the children from Teheran. Before the German army succeeded in occupying the whole of Poland 14,000 Jews had managed to get away; among them were 800 children between seven and fourteen and forty babies. They travelled on foot through the Ukraine, Siberia, Turkestan, Uzbekistan, and Persia, stumbling half-naked through trackless forests and deserts, plagued by disease and vermin and always hungry. In Teheran they were taken care of by the American Red Cross and, for some reason unknown, the British authorities granted them entry visas and they were flown to Palestine.

There were some clear-eyed people who realized in the 1930s that there was no future for Jews in Germany, but that there was hope for those children and young people who could be got out. Out of this vision grew the Youth Aliyah, and its prophetess was Henriette Szold. This remarkable woman was a native of Hungary, where she had been born in 1860, so sharing both year and country of birth with Theodor Herzl, whose work she strikingly supplemented. During most of her life Henriette Szold had lived in America, where she had founded the Hadassah, one of the leading Jewish relief organizations, with the care of women and children as its object. As the Biblical Sarah gave birth to a son in her old age, so Henriette Szold in her seventy-fourth year became mother to a generation of Israelis. It was she who built up the Youth Aliyah, an organization which got thousands of young people out of Germany and had them educated in neighbouring countries or trained for future employment in Palestine. Many of them worked on Dutch, Danish, and Swedish farms before becoming pioneers in their new home. Altogether the Youth Aliyah brought 100,000 boys and girls to Palestine, including Ephraim. Henriette Szold is reverenced by the Jewish people as the British reverence Florence Nightingale.

When Germany surrendered and Labour formed the first post-war Government in Britain it was generally believed that the gates of Palestine would now be opened to survivors of the concentration camps. In the event, British policy, under Ernest Bevin, was made even more restrictive and the Aliyah Beth even more necessary. The story of its work is more exciting than any thriller. Emissaries from Palestine were active in every country in Europe, gathering the refugees into camps, training them, providing them with false papers, passing them across frontiers, and reassembling them in secret camps in Italy. Radio connections were established between Tel Aviv and the various centres in Italy, and from that moment it was possible to co-ordinate the various operations. The Jewish Legion in the British Army was able to assist. With the inevitable disintegration of army conditions after a victory, they found it an easy matter to obtain material from depots. Army vehicles were 'borrowed' for transporting the refugees; specially difficult operations were carried out by false army units. Fleets of blockade-runners passed through the Mediterranean with illegal immigrants. Many of these ships were intercepted by British warships and their passengers interned in Cyprus, but others got through. They were received at selected points on the coast of Palestine by members of the Haganah and escorted by devious routes to *kibbutzim* where, furnished with false papers, they mingled with the original inhabitants. The Haganah worked desperately on these nocturnal operations, blowing up radar stations so that approaching vessels could not be observed, and blocking roads by means of land mines.

May 14, 1948, the day which saw the birth of Israel, marked a turning-point in the history of Jewish immigration into Palestine. The White Paper of 1939 with all its restrictions at once became void. From then on any Jew, wherever he might live, was welcomed.

Arriving in Haifa early in 1950 on my first visit to Israel, I found a bustle and a commotion such as I had never before experienced. It was like arriving in another and more primitive world. I was surrounded by swarms of people: mothers with their laughing or crying children holding on to their skirts or being dragged along behind them; long-bearded men with tired eyes staggering under heavy burdens; a young man who carried in his arms an old man who could have been his grandfather. They were shouting and laughing and crying; and wherever I looked I saw sweating and excited people, conscious only of one thing, that they were coming home. Some were so moved that they fell on their faces and kissed the ground. Even the dirty cobbles of Haifa to them meant *Eretz Israel*, the land above all others. A big immigrant ship had just unloaded its living cargo of a couple of thousand people. On many a Christmas Eve I have read in my church the prophecy of Isaiah: 'Thy sons shall come from afar off, and thy daughters be borne on their arms.' In the port that day it all came true before my very eyes.

In the following months I learnt that on such a day as this one could see people whose adventures had been incredible. Again and again I returned to Haifa when the ships were arriving. It was a sight I never tired of watching.

One day, after a passenger ship had docked with some of the last of the displaced persons from German concentration camps, my eye fell on a man who had evidently been in the country for some time. At least he had come from the direction of the city, as if he might have some errand there in the port. An oldish, bearded Jew, he had the pale, unhealthy complexion of a man who had spent years in a concentration camp. Dressed in shabby clothes, he shuffled along and his eyes were tired.

Suddenly it was as though he had been struck by lightning. For a few seconds his whole body trembled, then he raised himself to his full height and stood rigid, his head leaning back and with one arm raised. He stood in this grotesque position as though carved out of wood. I think that I gaped when I saw it. What had come over the man? Was it sunstroke? Then, following his gaze, I saw, fifty yards away, a woman of about his own age. She, too, stood, as though paralyzed.

Ten seconds can seem like an eternity; and for that length of time the two figures stood rigid. Then both cried out, their bodies relaxed, and they ran towards each other, limping and hopping. They clung together as if nothing should part them. I got their story. They were man and wife and they had lived in a small town in eastern Germany. On the 'Crystal Night' in November 1938 the Brownshirts had burst into their home, and they had been brutally treated and bundled into separate carts. They had heard no more of each other from that day on, and both had assumed that the other was dead—until the day in Haifa when the wife had arrived with some of the last survivors. Yes, indeed, human destinies can be studied in the port of Haifa.

Exodus in reverse, this mass immigration into Israel might be called. By 1951 the population had doubled and was 1,500,000. Now it is over 2,000,000 and is rapidly approaching 3,000,000. The hundreds of thousands of new Israelis come from more than seventy countries in practically every part of the world. News of Israel's independence penetrated to the remotest of Jewish communities, and everywhere men and women arose and set out, overcoming incredible obstacles and enduring inhuman hardships on the way. Whole communities in Europe and the East have been taken there by sea and air. Many strange stories can be told of them.

The Yemenite Jews were among the first to return. In the motley pattern of people from all the world they impart a tone of tender beauty that is impressive and very memorable. They are dark with olive-brown complexions, and have slender figures and dreamy, wistful eyes. The men wear long, thin beards; the women wear their jet-black hair in elaborate plaits and have vividly coloured embroidered gowns. They have many children. The Yemen is the country near Aden in the south-western

corner of Arabia. It is not known when or why the Jews
first settled there, but there is a legend that the Queen of
Sheba asked Solomon to send her some people who could mine
silver and gold, and another legend that after the destruction
of the Northern Kingdom in 722 B.C. the tribe of Gad roamed
the desert and eventually arrived in the Yemen where they
stayed. Yet a third legend says that when Cyrus permitted the
Jews of Babylon to return to Jerusalem Ezra also summoned his
kinsmen in the Yemen, and that when they refused he condemned them to live in perpetual poverty.

If this is so, the punishment was fulfilled, for under Islam
the Jews were treated as an inferior race and passed through
troubled times. They were forbidden to own weapons and
excluded from public office. They paid the value of a fifth of
their property in tax every year; their houses had to be lower in
height than Moslem houses; they had to ride side-saddle; and
they were obliged to pass Moslems on the left, which is the
side of the Devil. Jewish orphans were adopted by the authorities and brought up as Moslems. Most Jews were artisans,
skilled at beating gold and silver and weaving fine embroidery.
Others were small traders, but none was permitted to farm land,
let alone possess it. They lived a religious life, with the Sabbath
and the festivals as climaxes, the days between them being
regarded as night. Israel is glad of her Yemenites; they are
efficient and reliable, and ninety-six per cent are of more than
average intelligence. Sociologists are studying their culture and
traditions, because when people have lived for two and a half
millennia in isolation, as they have done, there are interesting
survivals.

News of the State of Israel gave rise to strong emotion in the
Yemen. From time immemorial the Yemenite Jews had waited
for the call to return home, and they now felt that the Mes-
sianic age had come. Asked why they were so eager to go, they
replied: 'We failed to answer the call from Ezra and were
punished by thousands of years in exile. We have heard that
David Ben-Gurion the Messiah has come, and we dare not
repeat our mistake.' The Jewish authorities opened negotiations

with the Imam of Yemen and the British in Aden and consent was obtained for the transfer of 45,000 Yemenite Jews. From their remote villages they walked through the desert, leaving all their belongings behind them except for their treasured *Torah*. At Aden airport they found the 'great bird' waiting to take them in its belly to Israel, and they entered it with singing and thanksgiving on their lips and were borne on its wings to the promised land. I saw one of these planes arrive. One of the last passengers to alight was a young man carrying his great-great-grandfather, a man of 112. He had carried him the 150 miles across the desert. The old man gave one look at the land of Israel, which proved to be his last; his head sank and he was dead. He had just succeeded in keeping the flickering flame of life alight long enough to see the place he had daily longed and prayed for.

The repatriation of the Yemenites was called Operation Flying Carpet. The return of the Iraqi Jews was known as Operation Ali Baba. Both names come from *A Thousand and One Nights*, and indeed the 'ransom of the prisoners of Zion' has much of the character of a fairy-tale. It was in the year 586 B.C. that King Nebuchadnezzar captured Jerusalem and carried its people off into exile in the country which we now call Iraq, but which was then called Babylonia. 'By the rivers of Babylon, there we sat down, yea, we wept, when we remembered Zion,' says the 137th Psalm. After seventy years of exile, the great King Cyrus allowed the Jews to return home and rebuild Jerusalem and its temple. They were led by Zerubbabel, and the poet of the Psalms sang: 'When the Lord turned again the captivity of Zion, we were like them that dream.' But it was only a small number who returned to the Holy City; the great majority stayed behind in Babylon, where they formed a large colony and attained to a high level of civilization. There were great prophets in Babylon; most of the Talmud was collected there; and the Jewish colleges were centres of learning. The Jews were also outstanding in social affairs. World-wide Jewish businesses had their headquarters in Babylon, and Jewish industry and ingenuity were valuable assets.

The old association of Jews and Arabs in Iraq came to a sudden
end and during and after the war between Israel and her
neighbours those Jews who were unfortunate to be living in
Arab countries paid the penalty. Resentment against them was
particularly marked in Iraq; anti-Jewish feelings ran high and
it was resolved to expel them. It was officially announced that
all Jews who wished to leave for Israel should register and be
out of the country by May 31, 1951. At the beginning of the
period there were long queues outside the offices and 100,000
people registered their names. The first emigrants were granted
fairly reasonable conditions and could take belongings up to the
value of fifty pounds. Soon, however, the conditions were made
stricter; the last to leave were refugees rather than emigrants.
When a Jew registered for emigration he at once sacrificed his
civil rights and was without protection. If he was an employee
he lost his job; if he kept a shop it was closed. If the Government had not been aware that the Jews were vital to the economy
of Iraq, they soon realized it. Economic activities were paralyzed.
To take one example: the majority of bank clerks had been
Jews, and when they were dismissed the bank services collapsed.
But the Government did not allow such considerations to
interfere with their intentions: rather ruin than Jews, seemed
to be its motto.

What took place in Iraq was a further Jewish disaster, which
was grimly reminiscent of Germany in the 1930s. There was
one big difference, however. There had been nowhere for the
German Jews to go between 1933 and 1945; but in 1951 the
Iraqi Jews were able to find a refuge in Israel. In Operation Ali
Baba they were flown from Baghdad to Lydda, in a vast airlift
which involved taking 120,000 passengers a distance of 1000
miles. The operation was successful and nobody was left
behind; but the majority arrived in a wretched condition,
displaying the marks of their experience and needing all the
help that could be given to them. The Iraqi Jews have proved
to be made of excellent material. They were a highly developed
Oriental community, which included many able and well-
educated people: intellectuals, bankers, businessmen, and many

artisans. They have remained a community in Israel, where whole quarters are now inhabited by Iraqi Jews.

Other Oriental communities also responded to the call. There have been many immigrants from Persia. Cochin Jews have come from India; a large community of *falasha*, almost negroid in appearance, is expected from Abyssinia; others are coming from Afghanistan and Shanghai.

Outstanding alongside the Yemenite and Iraqi Jews by reason of their numbers and conspicuous characteristics are the North African Jews. Jews have lived in Libya, Tripolis, Tunis, Algeria, and Morocco since the destruction of Jerusalem, many of them under primitive conditions. In Tripolis there were the cave-dwellers. For thousands of years these people had lived 900 feet below ground, in houses carved out of the rock. During the day the men worked for Arab farmers, or as pedlars, and during the night they locked themselves in behind iron doors in their caves. Only the dead went to rest near the surface; the living inhabited the earth beneath them. This entire community has been brought home to Israel, jumping from the Middle Ages to the Atomic Age.

Unrest in French North Africa has had repercussions on the Jews, who in civil wars invariably find themselves between the hammer and the anvil. The French accuse them of helping the rebels; the Nationalists say they side with the French. Efforts have therefore been made to rescue them, the more so since the conditions under which they have lived in North Africa, especially Morocco, have always been primitive. A typical example is that of the *Mellah* at Casablanca (*Mellah* is Arabic for 'Jewish quarter'). Separated from the rest of the city by a fence, the houses here are little more than caves, the better ones having two rooms but the great majority only one room without windows. The occupants sleep on rough wooden benches, often eight and ten to the room. There are no sanitary arrangements, and the stench is indescribable.

Worst of all, they enjoy no sort of legal protection and live in perpetual fear of violence and injustice from their Arab neighbours. The owner of the houses in which they live, and to whom they pay good rents, gets fun out of annoying them. Should a tenant complain, the owner will procure false witnesses to declare that he has cursed Islam, with probable ill effects. Prolonged insecurity has rendered the Jew apathetic, prone to allow things to take their own course. The misery and apathy are transmitted to the children.

Israel has found a mission here, and so far has brought home a few thousand North African Jews. However, they constitute a serious problem, since many of them are extremely primitive, knowing nothing of sanitary arrangements and eating utensils, and sleeping under the bed. Their mental apathy is an even greater obstacle, and it is almost impossible to talk to them; if one is addressed, they will reply in chorus. Psychologists and social workers are endeavouring to transform these 'problem children' into normal citizens, and have already achieved much, especially in the case of young people who have served in the army, and who in the Sinai campaign bore themselves like true soldiers.

The great Aliyah takes its picturesque and conspicuous features from the Orientals. But the great river also has tributaries in Europe. It drew, first of all, from the survivors of German concentration camps and the displaced persons in internment camps in Cyprus. The call was also heard by many Jews in countries which in spite of the German occupation had escaped 'the final solution'. Nearly all the Jews of Bulgaria and Yugoslavia have gone to Israel. The overwhelming majority of Polish Jews perished in the extermination camps, but some managed to escape to the Russian side. Many of these were repatriated to Poland, but preferred to emigrate. A fair number have gone to Israel. A few hundred thousand Hungarian Jews escaped, some emigrated, and many others escaped after the unsuccessful rising.

The central railway station in Vienna has been a stage on the Aliyah in recent years. In the autumn of 1958 trainloads of refugees began to arrive there from Rumania. It had been a long time since the last Rumanian Jews had come this way.

Immediately after the foundation of the State of Israel the Rumanian Government had allowed many to emigrate, but later it had changed its mind. In October 1958 it had announced unexpectedly, and without any explanation, that Jews could now register for emigration, and 125,000 had at once done so. Most of these were young people, their average age being less than forty.

There was naturally some speculation about the reasons for this decision; for a satellite of Russia does not act without her consent. Possibly the Kremlin meant it as a flick of the whip for Nasser: a warning to stop flirting with the United States. Possibly there were pressing domestic reasons. It is a fact that many Rumanian Jews occupied positions which required an academic education, and now there was a new generation of Rumanian intellectuals waiting to take over. Another possible explanation is that with 100,000 fewer people there would be more housing available for the rest. It is one way of solving a housing shortage without bricks and labour. Whatever the reason, the Jews were allowed to go; but they had to leave most of their belongings, including travel cases, behind them. Determined not to take any risks, the authorities told the emigrants to obtain the authorized packing cases, which excluded the possibility of smuggling.

So the trains began to rumble and the first Rumanian Jews arrived in Vienna and were helped on to Israel, where the Government had made preparations for their reception. Over 200,000 were expected during the year, and every available means was mobilized to meet the requirements. Urgent appeals went out to world Jews for financial aid. In Israel itself an immigration loan was floated, and as the proceeds were inadequate an extra tax was levied. All these efforts could have been spared, for the stream of refugees from Bucharest slowed down and soon stopped.

Just as quickly and unexpectedly as Rumania had opened the floodgates, she closed them again, and she gave no explanation. The Rumanian Ambassador to Israel refused to make any statement, and the Foreign Ministry in Bucharest refuses to discuss the matter with the Israeli Ambassador. Two things are certain, however: the Rumanian authorities now have a list of 'unreliable elements', and many families have been split up. Some of their members got across the frontier in time; others were to have been on the next train.

It will be readily understood that Israel was shouldering a heavy burden. A small and neglected country was suddenly receiving more immigrants than its existing population, averaging 600 a day during the first few years, while providing food, clothing, housing, services, schools, hospitals, libraries. She found it necessary to improvise, and of course she made mistakes.

During the first few years the immigrants were housed in large, primitive camps, where they were maintained at subsistence level until they could be found work. The British camps came in useful for this. In other places the immigrants had to be satisfied with tents, and these are unpleasant places to live in in winter. Even the provision of tents was a problem. A further disadvantage was that the camps were in out-of-the-way places, remote from centres of possible employment. Some other means of accommodation had to be found.

The solution was the *ma'abarah*—the word means 'transit', and so a *ma'abarah* is a transit camp. The transit camps are always near to growing industrial centres or new farming areas. Employment is thus on the doorstep, as it were. That, however, is the only thing that can be said in favour of the transit camps. They are not beautiful, just a clutter of wooden shacks; hot and stuffy in summer, wet and muddy in winter. Still, they are only temporary and each family spends its spare time building a house of its own in the vicinity. A site is allotted, architects' plans are provided, and loans are advanced by the authorities, so that a family is able to move into its own substantially built and serviceably arranged house at the earliest opportunity.

The transit camp is only an emergency measure, and as supplies improve a new system is being introduced, known as 'From ship to village.' Before ever the ship arrives at Haifa the immigrants' abilities and desires are discussed with them, together with the available possibilities. They are met by coaches on arrival and taken to a settlement of their choice. Here everything is waiting for them—house, furniture, land, livestock, implements. The next morning the family can begin a new life: the man in the fields, his wife in the kitchen, their children at school.

The number of immigrants has been much less in recent years than it was at the start; where before there were tens of thousands, there are now thousands. Even so there is a problem, and of course huge sums have been spent on this great undertaking. A greater problem than the financial cost, however, is the one of integrating and assimilating so many different types. It is fascinating to see how Israel is tackling this problem.

It was on one of the 'flying birds' which were taking Yemenite Jews to Israel. The pilot had the shock of his life when he looked round at his passengers. One of the women had made a fire on the floor and was quietly cooking a meal in her usual way. The story is characteristic of the inability of primitive people to understand all that is new in modern Israel. The Moroccans have never seen matches before and are unfamiliar with knives and forks, to say nothing of machinery and road safety.

'East is East and West is West, and never the twain shall meet.' But in Israel, in every town and village, almost under every roof, East and West meets and has to live together. Down to 1948 the European element was easily the biggest among the immigrants, but now the Oriental one predominates. For as long as the Russian Jews are prevented from emigrating and Western European, and more especially American, Jews are reluctant to exchange a life in comfort for a pioneer life in the land of their forefathers, the balance of population will continue to shift in favour of the Orientals. This may prove to be a dangerous development.

A foreigner in Israel visited a transit camp which was inhabited almost entirely by Orientals. Two small boys were playing with a ball and a man walked up to them and took their ball away, whereupon the boys started to cry and ran complaining to their father. Later that day the same man entered a *kibbutz* which was full of *Yekkes*—that is, German Jews, so called because, in a country of shirt-sleeves, they wear jackets. The same scene took place: the man again took a ball from the boys. But this time the boys refused to submit, and cried: 'You've no right to take our ball!'

The story illustrates the difference between the Western and the Eastern approach. The Oriental patiently submits to his fate. When locusts strip his fields, when fires rage and the drought and the flood destroy his crops he complains but does nothing about it. The Westerner fights back. There is the same sharp contrast in the general mental outlook of the two groups. The Oriental is meditative; he has time to wait; and though many religious leaders of the Orient urge work upon their disciples, what we call energy and drive are singularly hard to find. Of course everyone wants worldly goods, but unless they can be got with little effort they will do without them. 'What man is rich? He who is content with his allotted portion.'

Which of the two will turn out to be the stronger: the purposeful, mechanized Western civilization, or the reflective philosophy of the East? Actually, the question is wrongly phrased; for neither should dominate the other. On the contrary, they should supplement each other; if they do, if they arrive at the right synthesis, then the world will receive new inspiration from the old land of the Jews. Some time, East and West must meet.

Ben-Gurion is a man of visions, and this is one of them:

'From among the ragged children whom we have saved from a Moroccan *Mellah* there will come, perhaps, a new Spinoza. I live for the day when a Yemenite immigrant will be elected President of Israel.'

VIII

DESERT INTO GARDEN

❧

THE rain: where is it? The farmer anxiously surveys the sky for a sign of cloud, but it remains as blue as ever. Will he have to plough in the withered crops once again? This is the Negev, where rainless winters have wrought serious havoc.

Perhaps the farmer thinks of the story in the Talmud of Honi Hame'agel, the drawer of circles. Honi was given his nickname 2000 years ago when he reproached God for being silent to his prayers. He drew a circle round himself on the ground outside the synagogue and swore to stay inside it until rain came, and according to the legend God at last relented and sent the rain. It is said that during a recent winter, the driest in living memory, devout men met at Safad in emulation of Honi. They drew a circle and to the blowing of the ram's horn stood in the middle of it and said their prayers and chanted their psalms. It actually began to rain, and rained so heavily that they hastened to beg God not to take them too literally! Water has been the key to life in the Negev ever since time immemorial.

In northern Europe we usually have too much rain and too little sunshine; in Israel it is the other way round. Whereas Denmark has an average annual rainfall of twenty-five inches, the northern Negev has less than eight inches and the southern Negev, round Eilat on the Gulf of Aqaba, less than an inch. It would be a good thing if, with other commodities, we could exchange rain and sunshine!

In Israel there is no rain between April and the end of October

—the whole of the summer half-year. Coming from a country where the only certain thing about the weather is its uncertainty, one finds it strange that the sun should shine daily for six months on end. One begins to appreciate the grumble of the labourers in the vineyard: 'us, which have borne the burden and heat of the day'. If, moreover, there is a *hamsin* blowing, then the limit is reached. The *hamsin* is an east wind, of which we read in the Bible that it is one of the greatest of all afflictions. It is a dry, hot desert wind, full of invisible dust and electricity which make people irritable and bad-tempered. It is said that if an Arab goes amuck and cuts his wife's throat on the fifth day of a *hamsin* he will be exonerated.

A spring has always been a place of importance, as we see in the Bible. People would settle by a spring and name their town or village after it. A tourist guide to Palestine contains no fewer than thirty-five names in the index beginning in *Ain*, which is Hebrew for 'spring'. Wells were equally important, and there are many place-names beginning in *Beer*, which means 'well', notably Beersheba, the capital of the Negev. 'And Abraham came to Beersheba and dug a well.' Abraham's well may still be seen at Beersheba, along with six other wells. The name Beersheba means 'Seven Wells'. The ancients took care to preserve their water; they made cisterns for catching the rain and they built aqueducts to lead it into their towns. Irrigation was a familiar art even in those days, the winter streams being dammed and the water stored for summer use. In the Negev there are remains of water-mains which show that the water was led uphill to the vineyards on the mountain slopes.

Installations such as these must be maintained and cared for, and they have been neglected. The Arabs and the Turks left them to decay for centuries. The cisterns gradually silted up, the terraces deteriorated, the fertile top soil drifted with the wind or was washed away by the rain; the erosion left only a dry and stony landscape behind. In the time of Christ it is estimated that Palestine had 5,000,000 inhabitants; a census in 1850 showed only 50,000.

When I first visited the Negev, in 1950, it was a desert, dead and empty except in cultivated patches, and Beersheba was a small and dusty place of 500–600 inhabitants. I saw it again from the air five years later, when there was a network of new settlements and villages with roads leading to them; the land itself was chequered with fields, brown where they had been newly ploughed, green under growing crops, yellow with the harvest. I had never thought that I should live to see the fulfilment of Isaiah's prophecy that the desert would become a garden. In those five years, of course, Israel had brought water to the Negev.

Taking a lesson from the ancients, they began by damming the wadis which had carried off the winter rains and storing the water in vast reservoirs. This is not enough, and more modern methods are now being applied. Engineers, using modern hydrological and geophysical appliances, among them radio-direction finders, have located subterranean rivers which carried off the flow of rainwater from the mountains of Judaea to the sea. Instead of making a series of costly drillings at random, it is now possible to go straight to the sources. The first major step towards bringing water to the Negev is the Yarkon project.

The Yarkon and the Jordan are the only rivers in Israel which do not dry out in the summer. The Yarkon flows into the Mediterranean at Tel Aviv, and though only ten to twelve miles long carries a large volume of water. All this water was wasted, but now engineers are diverting the river so that three-quarters of the water will flow south. A huge pumping station draws off the flood water and pumps it through vast piping systems some sixty miles to the Negev, where it is distributed to thousands of irrigation centres.

Not even this will be adequate in the long run, and indeed the Yarkon is only one among many projects. The Jordan is capable of a much bigger yield, but in this case foreign policy is involved. Unlike the Yarkon, the Jordan flows through other countries besides Israel. Before its waters can be harnessed, there will have to be an agreement with the Lebanon, Syria, and Jordan.

The Jordan is a fast-flowing river; indeed the name means 'flowing down'. Its chief sources are in the snow-capped mountains of Hermon, 10,000 feet above sea-level, and it flows into the deepest gorge in the world, the Dead Sea, which is 1290 feet below sea-level at its surface. In its 100-mile course it falls farther than any other river in the world. It is not a large river, and is smaller than I had imagined it to be. Nor am I the only person who has been disappointed. There was once a Russian pilgrim, who had spent his life on the banks of the Volga and had always longed for the Jordan. After many years of planning, he eventually set out to see it, and walked all the way there. But when he arrived at the Jordan he felt so let down, because it could not compare with the Volga, that he drowned himself in it. The distance from Gennesaret to the Dead Sea is only about sixty miles, but if the river were to be straightened out it would be 180 miles long, so much does it twist and turn. It is full of eddies, rapids, and small waterfalls, and is brown and muddy; its banks are a jungle. The Jordan looks finest at the point where it leaves the Lake of Gennesaret, that glistening, sunlit expanse backed to the north by the snowy peak of Mount Hermon, called by the Arabs Jebel-esh-Sheikh—the Mountain Sheikh. Israel's water projects chiefly involve the stretch of the Jordan between Hermon and Gennesaret.

At this point Israel projects an arm, the northern point of Galilee, to Metulla on the Lebanese border. Here is the wide Huleh Valley between the mountains of the Lebanon and Syria, where the Jordan rises. The valley takes its name from the Lake of Huleh, the site of the waters of Merom and Joshua's defeat of the King of Hazor. Down to a few years ago the problem in the Huleh Valley was the reverse of the problem in the Negev. There, there was a surplus of water, and the Jordan's springs broadened out into sour swamps surrounding the lake. It was picturesque scenery with shoulder-high forests of papyrus, yellow water-lilies floating on the still water, and a rich fauna; but the land was waterlogged and mosquitoes rendered the whole valley uninhabitable.

The Huleh Valley is one of the regions of Israel that have been made fertile in the course of a few years. It was a transformation which began in 1939 when pioneers settled there. Defying the malaria and the intense heat, they have made the desert grow and are making a determined onslaught on the swamps. The Huleh Valley is now a good agricultural district offering scope for tens of thousands of new settlers. The venture did not succeed without friction. Syria did what she could to obstruct the work, and Israel suffered heavy losses not only from disease but also from Syrian bullets.

The greatest of the Israeli water projects has yet to be tackled. This is the plan to link the Jordan with the Negev by the construction of a canal from the river to the Lake of Gennesaret. When this has been accomplished, the problem of irrigating the Negev will have been solved. The whole character of the country will have been changed and immense possibilities are involved in the plan.

As already stated, however, the waters of the Jordan are shared with some of Israel's Arab neighbours, and they are opposed to her economic development. In 1955 President Eisenhower sent his technical adviser, Mr Eric Johnston, to the Middle East in order to negotiate with the Governments in question. An agreement had almost been reached when, at the last moment, the Arab League changed its mind. The opposition can be described by no other word but 'sabotage'. The river flows to no avail into the Dead Sea, and Syria and Jordan would also benefit from its exploitation. But, as an Arab leader has expressed it:

'Though we were to get ninety-nine per cent of the Jordan's water and Israel only one, we would fight the project tooth and nail because of this one per cent.'

In the circumstances Israel declared herself entitled to proceed with the Johnston plan and is now working on it, drilling through mountains, laying pipes. Reservoirs have already been provided. It is expected that the locks can be opened in 1968.

Meanwhile, the Arab States are contemplating counter-measures, one of which would divert two of the Jordan's tributaries away from Israel. As usual, however, they cannot agree among themselves.

It is always possible that further friction will be avoided by the solution of a problem that has engaged the minds of men for centuries, the problem of removing the salt from sea-water. Research on this is going on in Israel, and provisional reports are optimistic.

Some years ago the Jewish actor Edward G. Robinson paid a visit to Israel. In the course of conversation with President Weizmann he expressed pleasure at the luxuriant oases he had seen in the desert.

'Desert?' Weizmann said. 'There are no deserts here.' And he went on:

'The poet Haim Nahman Bialik said that when our people were driven out of Palestine God covered the land with large stones and sand so as to camouflage it and lead others into thinking that it was valueless and so to staying away. Bialik was right. All that our country needs now is the removal of the camouflage—with a little sweat.'

The Negev and the Huleh Valley are not the only two areas where this removal is taking place. Along the central coast lies the Plain of Sharon, which was reclaimed from malaria swamps at the beginning of the century. The same has happened in the Jezreel Valley. In recent years groups of settlements have been growing up in the 'corridor' which leads to Jerusalem. Operation Lahish shows how a large co-ordinated national scheme can be realized. Lahish stands about midway between Jerusalem and Gaza, where the mountains shelve down to the coastal plain, near to the Jordan border. The town was a frontier fort in the Kingdom of Judah and we read of it in the Bible; Nebuchadnezzar besieged and captured it in the 580s B.C.

before turning on Jerusalem. Despatches from officers to the commandant at Lahish in the last war of Judah, written on potsherds, have been found in the *tel*.

Where a few years ago the landscape was barren and stony a new town is growing up, with satellites, and round these, in turn, new settlements and villages are arising. This is regional planning; large areas are being reclaimed, chiefly for growing industrial crops such as cotton and groundnuts, and other areas are being laid down as pasture. In the central town, which stands near to the *tel* that covers the Philistine town of Gath (hence the name Kirjat Gat, 'City of Gath') cotton mills are now operating. Kirjat Gat will be a modern city, with multi-storey blocks, a supermarket, cinemas, and community centres. As Operation Lahish approached completion a similar project was launched a little to the north-east, in the Abdullam area. These undertakings form part of the 'strategic settlement', which has the dual purpose of reclamation and national defence.

An old country is being rejuvenated, but at the same time the people are returning to old ways. In the Biblical period the Israelites were farmers. During the long centuries of exile, however, they lost their contact with the soil. Jews were forbidden to own land and were driven to urban life. Now the flow is in the other direction. Every year tens of thousands of immigrants settle on the land; it is a bold enterprise because hardly any of them know anything about farming. They have to be instructed and advised, and of course in the first difficult years the authorities have to assist them. But the step must be taken. Barren fields must be cultivated. It is a case of planning not for tomorrow, but for future generations and future centuries. One important aspect of the whole problem is the psychological revolution which is rapidly transforming the people of the ghetto into modern farmers.

Of course, some of the settlers fail and go back to the towns; but four-fifths of them have persisted and have become efficient farmers. Country life comes as a matter of course to their children. With them a new generation of farmers is growing up.

There is a celebrated passage in Deuteronomy which describes the promised land and the seven crops which grow in it:
'A land of wheat, and barley, and vines, and fig trees, and
pomegranates; a land of oil olive and honey.' All these are
shown on a set of Israeli stamps that was issued to com-
memorate the Jewish New Years of 5719 and 5720, which
correspond to 1958 and 1959. They are still important products
of Israeli agriculture, though agricultural experiments have
discovered other promising crops. The production of citrus
fruits—oranges, grapefruit, and lemons—is famous. Almonds,
bananas, cotton, sugar beet, potatoes, and groundnuts are other
good crops. Then there are flowers. A few years ago when the
Dutch tulip crop failed the Dutch imported Israeli bulbs,
which they were also able to re-export. Dairy cows, sheep, and
poultry are abundant, but pigs are rare, because the Law of
Moses classes them as unclean animals.

The perpetual problem remains that of water. Crops that
are not irrigated will fail in time of drought. More important
even than water, however, is the human material, and by means
of the *kibbutzim* Israel has succeeded in creating the right type
of men and women for the country's rejuvenation.

The immigrants of the first Aliyah established their settlements in a ring round Jaffa. They came from Russia and Poland
and the settlements were true copies of the unsightly, untidy
villages they had left. They were new to farming in the Israeli
climate and unaccustomed to hard physical labour, and it did
not occur to them to train for it: they employed cheap Arab
labour. They fared badly, and but for the help of benefactors
like Baron Edmond de Rothschild and Baron Moritz de Hirsch
they would all have gone bankrupt.

The people of the second Aliyah, those who arrived after the
abortive revolution of 1905 and who were confirmed Socialists
(among them Ben-Gurion), were moved by a new spirit. Their
motto was 'Conquest by work', and they asserted that the land
could not be won except by the labour of Jews. Academic and
commercial students, they intended to begin a new era in

Jewish life and wipe out the memory of 2000 years of unnatural urban existence. They believed that their people should return to the life of their ancestors in harmony with nature and in association with animals and crops. Their ideals found their clearest expression in the *kibbutz*.

Kibbutz means 'together'. The idea is that those who choose to live in a *kibbutz* belong together, each giving according to his means and receiving according to his needs. The members do their own work, outside labour being engaged only in special cases. They elect their various departmental managers from among themselves and the general assembly appoints men to the jobs for which they are found to be most suitable, either in the fields, on the farm, in the gardens, the kitchen, the laundry, workshops, or school. No wages are paid and all income is pooled; from house and food to cigarettes and postage stamps, each receives according to his needs. Education of children and the care of the sick and the aged are joint responsibilities. There is no private property, everything being held in common. Everyone eats in the dining-hall, where no one has his regular seat and all mix with newcomers, so that all get to know one another.

Children are brought up in nurseries and schools according to age and live, not with their parents, but collectively in children's homes, boys and girls together, up to the age of twelve. They spend the evenings and the Sabbath with their parents. Mothers can thus devote the whole of their time to the service of the *kibbutz*, all available labour therefore being concentrated on the main task of developing the economy.

Until I saw it, I must say that I had doubts about this side of the system. There are bonds of affection between parent and children which are essential to both, and one cannot help wondering if the result of collective education is mass-produced children. I have discussed the problems in scores of *kibbutzim* and asked many questions. The children I saw were fine and healthy, happy, and well dressed. If a woman passed the playground one or other of them was sure to call *Imma!* (Mother), and a moment after mother and child would be holding hands.

The natural family ties had not been broken. In talking to settlers the critic is likely to be asked: 'Why assume that a woman who can give birth to a child knows how to educate it?' Or: 'Don't you see that we have solved the problem of the only child?' Always the discussion will conclude with the reminder that parents and children are together when they are both free.

Some people would link the *kibbutz* system with Communism, but a *kibbutz* is quite different from a Russian *kolkhoz*. The *kibbutz* is a voluntary institution; anyone can leave it when he wants, and it is free from State supervision. The *kibbutzim* are Communist in the way that the primitive Christian communities, described in the Acts of the Apostles, were Communist: free associations of individuals in a fellowship of self-sacrifice. The object of the self-sacrifice is to achieve something which only a later generation will enjoy. It should be added, also, that there is no sort of regimentation or standardization in the life of a *kibbutz*, and that there is every kind of transitional form from the fully collective community to the loose association of individuals. The form which I have described is peculiar to Israel.

The *Rosh Hashanah*, the Jewish New Year, was celebrated in the year called by Christians 1955 on September 17th. The year was only six days old when *Kol Israel*, the 'Voice of Israel', announced that at noon that day, September 23rd, Dov Joseph, the Minister of National Development, would broadcast an important statement. Those who tuned in all over Israel were not disappointed by what the Minister had to tell.

The story has a long prelude. For years Israel had been prospecting for oil. The preliminary reports had been favourable; after all, Israel is located in the same part of the world as the rich oil countries of Iraq and Saudi Arabia. There was also other evidence that there might be oil in Israel. In ancient times asphalt from the Dead Sea had been exported to Egypt, where it was used for sealing mummy cases; and asphalt and oil are related products. The Bible, 'Israel's economic geography', also suggested the possibility of oil. Geologists pointed out that the probable cause of the destruction of Sodom and Gomorrah was an explosion of a reserve of natural gas. Where there is gas, they argued, there would probably be oil. Of course, there was always the possibility, as some sceptics objected, that any gas and oil which might have been present in the past would be there no longer. Still, most of the omens were favourable, and so drilling was undertaken and success was achieved.

In the late summer of 1955 a derrick was built near to the old Philistine town of Ashquelon, at a place called Heletz, and on September 17th gas was struck there at a depth of 5500 feet. The excitement of the engineers assembled on the platform above was intense. Would there also be oil? They had not long to wait. Suddenly, a column of oily black liquid rose sixty feet into the air and descended like an umbrella, almost smothering the engineers in its spray. Subsequent analyses showed the oil to be of good quality, like the oil of Kuwait. This was the great news which Dov Joseph had to impart.

Twelve o'clock arrived and the Minister duly appeared at the microphone. Then one of those incidents occurred which are typical of Israel. Instead of immediately giving the good news about the oil, the Minister began to chant the *Shehekejanu* thanksgiving: Praised be the Lord who hath brought us to this day. The news came after it. There was rejoicing throughout the nation; *Mazzel tov!* (Congratulations!) was heard both in the fields and in the city streets. It was as though Israel had won a victory, as in a sense she had: an important economic victory. The repercussions went round the world; that afternoon there was a rise in Israeli shares on the New York Stock Exchange and business was held up for two hours by the great demand for them.

The first 4000 feet of drilling at Heletz had been easy, for the Iraqi Oil Company of Britain had drilled there in the winter of 1947-8 but had then abandoned their operations, a few months before the British had left Palestine. One should never speculate as to what would have happened if history had taken another course, but it is sometimes difficult to refrain; and one cannot help wondering what the result would have been if the British company had gone on for another 1500 feet. Would the British Government, in that case, have relinquished the Mandate?

There are now a number of derricks at Heletz, which has been called 'the Texas of Israel'. Other wells have also been located, and a promising deposit has been found near the Dead Sea. In 1959, oil production totalled 120,000 tons. The wells at Heletz now supply ten per cent of Israel's requirements.

A word often seen on roadside posters in Israel is *delek*. The word means 'fuel', but as the only fuel that is used to any large extent is oil, when one says *delek* one usually means oil. There are other interesting developments in this field.

The British built large oil refineries at Haifa, to which the crude oil was brought by pipeline from Kirkuk in Iraq, with consequent saving in freight costs. When Israel became independent the oil was re-routed through Lebanon ports and for some years the refineries at Haifa were closed down. They recommenced operations after the Sinai campaign, when the Gulf of Aqaba was opened to Israeli shipping and the new port of Eilat was constructed. Israel at once began building a new pipeline from Eilat to Haifa; the crude oil is now shipped in giant tankers from Iran through the Red Sea and the Gulf of Aqaba to Eilat, where it is pumped through the pipeline to Haifa for refining. These new industries are of importance not only to Israel but also to Western Europe. Now Western Europe need no longer be dependent upon the Suez Canal. What is more, the route through Israel is cheaper.

The Dead Sea is also known as Yam Hamelah, which means 'Salt Sea'. It is an appropriate name. As already mentioned, it is 1290 feet below sea-level and is the deepest point in the world. In a fast car one feels the change in atmospheric pressure as one approaches it, just as one does in a descending aeroplane. There is no outfall from the Dead Sea; the Jordan flows into it and then stops. The fact that there is no flooding as a result is explained by the evaporation due to the intense heat, which

cancels out the inflow. One effect of this has been an accumula-
tion over the centuries of deposits of various salts, among them
potash, bromium, and magnesium. The deposits are sufficient
to meet world requirements of these chemicals for the next few
thousand years.

In the 1930s the Jews began to exploit this wealth; they built
a large plant at the northern end of the Dead Sea near Jericho,
with an annexe at Sodom in the south. The northern workings
were destroyed in the 1948 war when the place itself was lost
to Israel, but the other plant at Sodom has been developed.
Like so much else in Israel, this is only in its early stages, yet
hundreds of thousands of tons of chemicals are now extracted
every year. One day when the required supply of electricity is
available (a nuclear power station is planned at Sodom), the
production may attain to world dimensions. Already a road has
been built through the mountains of Judah from Sodom to
Beersheba, and a railway line has been projected which may be
taken on as far as Eilat, from where the products can be
exported to the Far East.

There are other sources of potential wealth besides oil and
chemicals. I have already quoted from Deuteronomy, and there
is a reference in the same book to 'a land whose stones are iron,
and out of whose hills thou mayest dig brass'. Again, we read
in the Bible that King Solomon's men mined copper at Ezion
Geber in the southern Negev, which is roughly the site of
modern Eilat. Copper was in those days a precious metal,
three measures being equal to one measure of gold. Some thirty
years ago an archaeologist succeeded in locating King Solomon's
copper mines, and miners are working there once more, using
modern equipment. Past and present have been linked. As an
engineer said:

'We sometimes feel that the last shift of King Solomon's men
have just dropped their picks and gone home.'

The iron deposits mentioned in Deuteronomy have also been
located, and the possibility of their exploitation is being
investigated. More important than these, however, are the
large deposits of phosphate in the Negev. There have been new

discoveries of silicon, ceramic clay, felspar, chaolin, gypsum, and manganese.

The industries of Israel have expanded rapidly during the few years in which she has existed. From the Mandate she inherited flourishing small industries in the towns and in *kibbutzim*, and these have been developed. Today she also has oil mills, margarine factories, canneries, a large cement industry, diamond-polishing works, spinning mills and clothing factories, and breweries, while sugar refining is being developed in pace with the expansion in the production of beet sugar. There has also been a rapid expansion in chemical manufactures, especially at the fertilizer works at Haifa, where potash and phosphates from the Dead Sea and the Negev are processed.

Building is proceeding on an immense scale. New immigrants have to be housed, and thousands of new dwellings have to be found and found quickly. The population of Tel Aviv is nearing 500,000; Haifa and Jerusalem are both growing fast; new centres are being built; Beersheba, which has 40,000 inhabitants now, is expected to reach 100,000. Furthermore, a modern town is being developed at Ashquelon; Kirjat Gat is growing just as fast; Asdod, a fishing town, will soon be Israel's fourth port after Haifa, Tel Aviv, and Eilat. As for the last-named town, this is bursting with industrial and constructional activity and its new harbour will soon be an important gateway to the East.

No other country is faced with such immense economic problems as this small new State with its hostile neighbours, its immigrants, its continual political ferment, its religious controversies, and its sore need of soil improvement. It is remarkable that Israel has survived at all. There were times when her imports were to her exports in the ratio of seven or eight to one; when half the revenue was required for defence; and when the State almost collapsed under the burden of immigration.

Nevertheless, she held her own and is now over the worst. Expanding exports, American grants in aid, gifts from Jews abroad, investments, Government loans, and

German indemnities: all have eased her difficulties. But her problems are still pressing; relief and indemnities cannot last for ever; in the long run she must become self-supporting.

The first four or five years were hard ones for the ordinary Israeli. All goods were rationed and scarce and near-famine conditions prevailed. It must be obvious that no country can absorb more immigrants than its entire population without all-round restrictions, and with its army on a war footing as well the strain on the economy becomes even greater. The pressures are now easing, as thrift and hard work begin to get their reward. There is a plentiful supply of goods and a wide choice in the shops.

It is a typically Jewish characteristic to make light of one's difficulties, just as it is a civilized trait to laugh at oneself. Self-irony helped the Jews over the horrors of persecution and the centuries of the ghetto, and its help was needed again in the early years of Israel. This is one of the stories they laughed at:

The Knesset was debating the economic situation and a member suggested that the problem might be solved by a declaration of war on America. 'They'll defeat us in a few days,' he said, 'and will have to treat us as they treated Germany and Japan: rehabilitate us and lend us millions of dollars.' The suggestion was applauded, but then a thoughtful little politician rose and said:

'But suppose we win?'

A laugh can smooth a rough journey. Chaim Weizmann expressed something greater when he spoke the famous words: 'In Israel we are realists; that is is why we believe in miracles.'

IX

WISDOM BUILT HERSELF A HOUSE

DOWN to a few years ago, Ramban Street on the Israel side of Jerusalem was a cul-de-sac. The Ramban, as it is conveniently called, is a fashionable villa road bisecting Rehavia, a district built in the twenties. The houses stand half-concealed behind luxuriant shrubberies and, like all Jerusalem, are built of stone quarried in the mountains of Judaea—grey, brown, ochre, occasionally pinkish. Rehavia is one of the select parts of Jerusalem, largely inhabited by University people. It was on the first occasion that my route had taken me through Ramban, a dozen years ago, that I had discovered it led no-where; or rather, that it ended in a stony and pathless waste. It was strange to walk along a pleasant, well-kept street and suddenly find oneself on the edge of the desert. One had to be something of an acrobat in order to climb down the great gap there. Behind it the view opened on to low, bare mountains. On a summer day the landscape was grey or brown with the drought; in spring the cliffs were a riot of wild flowers. On an eastward slope I saw stunted olive trees with silvery-grey, dusty leaves. Between them a shepherd was watching his flock, which incomprehensibly found sparse food among the stones.

The scenery was picturesque and ramblers enjoyed this near corner of the wilderness. But when, as often as I could, I went to where Ramban ends, it was in order to look down on the ancient monastery that for 1500 years has stood at the foot of the cliffs. Encircled by massive window-less walls, and sur-mounted by a church tower, it recalls a medieval fortress. The

Arabs call the gorge Wady el Mousallabe, or Valley of the Cross, and the monastery itself is known as the Monastery of the Sacred Cross. It gets its name because it stands, according to legend, on the spot where the Roman soldiers took the cypress from which they made the cross of Christ, the tree itself having been planted 1000 years before by Lot. Church and monastery are owned by the Greek Orthodox Patriarchate of Jerusalem and have suffered varying fortunes; capture, destruction, restoration are chapter headings in its long history. Arab warriors, crusaders, Mongols, Turks, British troops of Allenby's army: all have passed by or burst into it. The sight of the Monastery of the Sacred Cross in the ravine on the edge of Jerusalem's 'desert' moved and fascinated me. Here one sensed the sweep of history, of faith and human defiance of the ravages of nature and looting soldiers.

Today the past no longer holds sovereign sway over the Valley of the Cross. I know of few places in Israel where present and future have made the old into new to the same, almost startling, extent. The Ramban is no longer a cul-de-sac. Boldly the road runs out into the desert. A smooth and asphalted highway corkscrews down into the gorge, and climbing up the other side continues through a rocky landscape which only five years ago must have looked as the patriarchs of the Bible saw it. Where only a flock of sheep grazed, cars and buses whizz by. Their journey has an object. A mile or so farther on, on Givath Ram (which means High Hill), stand a group of monumental new buildings. This is the heart of modern Israel; one might add, of world Jewry: for it is the new Hebrew University. From the Middle Ages and barren nature it is only a couple of minutes by car to nuclear laboratories and research rooms where professors and undergraduates are studying some of man's greatest treasures. The new University also stands as evidence of the final chapter in the struggle for a centre for Jewish culture. Yet new as it is, it has already had to move. Its brief history will bear comparison for drama with the story of the old monastery in the desert at the end of Ramban Street.

When the first train after the 1948 war climbed the mountains of Judaea from Tel Aviv to Jerusalem it carried a double load of bread and books. In this there was something symbolical. Jerusalem had been besieged and almost starving, but now communications had been restored and supplies could get through to the capital without hindrance. They know, however, in Israel that man does not live by bread alone, and so by the first train they also sent books, some of the 70,000 volumes saved from Polish libraries that were intended for the students of Jerusalem University.

Before the First World War the founders of Zionism, notably Weizmann, had already had visions of the University which the Jewish people would one day expect to build in Jerusalem. They were conscious of the paradox of wanting to establish a centre of learning in a country where everything would have to start from scratch, and where the crying need would be for elementary things like ploughs, roads, and harbours. To Jews, however, there was nothing at all remarkable in this. With them, study and material advancement go hand in hand. Consequently, the technological sciences are connected with the study of Jewish lore and general humanist disciplines. Weizmann laid the foundations of the new University as long ago as 1918, when the war in Palestine was still in progress. The site was Mount Scopus, where Titus had had his headquarters in the year 70 during the siege of Jerusalem. Weizmann performed the initial ceremony to the accompaniment of distant gunfire.

By 1925 the first buildings stood complete and gleaming white in the sunshine. From the outset this was different from any other University, being not only the University of the people of this country but also belonging to and serving all Jews wherever they may live. World Jewry maintains and supports it, and world Jewry looks to it for guidance in intellectual and spiritual life. The University, for its part, sees as its prime objective the preservation and study of the Jewish way of life. Indeed, since the disaster of Europe and the destruction of the old centres of learning, it has become the natural focus of

Jewish science and scholarship, thus forming a bridge between Jerusalem and the people of the Dispersal. Consequently, the heart of the University is the Institute of Jewish Studies; the subjects studied are not only the Bible and the Talmud, but also Hebrew philology and literature, Jewish philosophy, mysticism, law, and history, as well as Palestinian archaeology; in short, everything connected with Jewish culture and civilization.

Two buildings stand out and are visible from afar: the Hadassah hospital and the library. The former performed an important service to both Jews and Arabs, for it was the centre for the campaign against what Weizmann called the twin plagues of Palestine: the dreadful eye diseases, and malaria. It took its name from the great Hadassah organization in America which has already been mentioned. The word means 'myrtle', which is a symbol of its idealistic aims. The library was a notable 'sight'. The collection of 120,000 Hebrew books is the largest in the world, and the department of Hebrew incunabulae (books printed before 1500) is remarkable for its size and quality, the library being one of the great repositories of these rare works. In addition, it possesses outstanding collections of Oriental books and a vast medical library. It is hardly necessary to say that the museum of Jewish antiquities is unequalled, as are the collections of Biblical and Talmudic botany.

The reader will have observed that I have spoken of the University on Mount Scopus in the past tense; in fact for the last twelve years these fine buildings have been empty and deserted. During the 1948 war the University was in the firing line; and after the tragic incident when a convoy of seventy doctors and nurses was ambushed and all were murdered, Mount Scopus was cut off from Jerusalem. The 1000 students were on military service, and it is largely to their credit that Jerusalem was held. Their casualties were heavy; one-tenth of them being killed and many severely wounded. The University itself was occupied by Jewish troops, who though isolated fought on. Mount Scopus is still Israeli territory, but it is an enclave in an Arab area and the road leading to it is barred.

A few men keep guard there, and once a week a United Nations convoy gets through with supplies.

Thus at the end of the war Israel found herself without a University, at the very time when she most needed one. A new civil service had to be built up; many immigrants required medical attention; there were many thousands of children to be educated. And there was a shortage of lawyers, doctors, and teachers. Though students and professors were available, there was an absence of suitable accommodation, while the 500,000 precious books on Mount Scopus were 'captives', inaccessible and unusable. Improvisation was necessary, and it had to be quick. The various faculties were therefore accommodated in former monasteries, schools, offices, and homes. Teaching and research took place in confined and unsuitable premises, and overcrowding was serious. But there was no alternative; work had to be done, and it was done with a will and with good humour.

While the work of the University went on, Israel planned to replace the buildings that had been lost. In 1954 work began at Givath Ram and it is now almost complete; though it was done at an impressive speed, there is no sign of haste in the result. The University is one of the most beautiful in the world, both as a whole and in its details. The faculties have now all been accommodated, with auditoria, laboratories, an administrative block, and halls of residence. The buildings have been mainly built from the stone that was blasted from the foundations, and many architects have collaborated in the work and left the marks of their personalities on it. One finds wonderful variety and assured taste, besides interesting individual features. The faculty of law is built on ten pillars symbolizing the ten commandments, and contains a judge's seat from Canada, the building being the work of Canadian Jews. Outside the faculty of economics there are two millstones, while in the administrative building there are mosaics from Galilee. The University synagogue is a fine example of modern architecture, bearing a remarkable resemblance to a mushroom. The University itself forms part of a larger scheme, which will include Ministerial buildings, among them the Foreign Ministry, besides the new Knesset, a congress hall, and a large museum centre.

More important than the thirty buildings of the University is of course the work that is done by the professors and the 4000–5000 undergraduates. The students are more mature than most of those at European and American universities, being mostly well up in their twenties before they begin studying. Both men and women have had their studies delayed by military service lasting from two to two-and-a-half years, and have also had to take part in manœuvres or undergo reserve training. What is more, they must have work, often full-time, in order to support themselves and in many cases a wife and family. It is not uncommon among the older students to find some who still bear the marks of German concentration camps or the Sinai campaign. At Givath Ram, too, one meets all sorts of unusual students, including members of the Knesset or senior military officers (General Moshe Dayan was, up to the election in 1959, one of these men), who in their youth were engaged in politics or defence and have only recently had the time to study. In recent years quite a number of young Arabs have entered the University and now study alongside Jewish Israelis. It is a promising sign that the two groups are coming together in the new State.

One of the University's most precious possessions is the collection of the seven Dead Sea scrolls. Their history is worth telling. In November 1947, just before the United Nations adopted the partitioning plan, Jerusalem was divided into two warring camps. Across the barbed-wire entanglements Professor E. L. Sukenik, the father of Yigal Yadin, negotiated with an Armenian antique dealer from Bethlehem. The two men had to stretch far before reaching each other. But the Armenian managed to pass a scrap of brown leather containing Old Hebrew letters to Sukenik and tell him that it was from one of seven parchment scrolls which he had bought from a shepherd, who in turn had found them in a cave near the Dead Sea. If the Professor would come to Bethlehem he could view the find, which was for sale. With a trained eye the professor of archaeology studied the leather and the lettering, and realized that the find was of the greatest importance and doubtless of great age. Hostilities were on the point of breaking out. To travel to Bethlehem would be to risk his life. Sukenik consulted his son, the general, as an expert. His reply was:

'If you ask me as a military man I must say that the journey may cost you your life. If you ask as a father asking a son I must beg you to stay at home. But if it is as one archaeologist to another, I say: "For heaven's sake, go!"'

Sukenik risked his skin and all went well. But he obtained only three of the scrolls. When he arrived in Bethlehem he found that the other four had already been sold to America. Sadly he wrote in his diary: 'The Jewish people have lost a precious inheritance.' The story, however, has a postscript, though unhappily Sukenik himself did not live to hear it, as he died a few years earlier. But during a journey in the United States Yigal Yadin learnt that the four scrolls had been put up for sale, at the fabulous price of $250,000. Yet he succeeded in raising the money, and now all seven of the scrolls are preserved in their obvious home, the Hebrew University of Jerusalem. Through them the scholars of modern Israel can listen over a gulf of 2000 years to the words and thoughts of their forefathers. Once again, the ancient past has become a living reality.

A gap greater than 2000 years separates the old University on Mount Scopus and the new one at Givath Ram. Though the actual distance between them is only a few miles, they are in a sense worlds apart. Israel, however, is convinced that it will not be for ever, and that, in one way or another, she will recover her lost University. Plans have been made for using it; and when the visitor asks what use the buildings will be put to 'if Israel recovers Mount Scopus', he always gets the same answer: '*Lo efshar—matai*.' ('Not if, but when.')

Thirty years ago, civilization came to an end at Rehovoth, which lies fifteen miles to the south of Tel Aviv. It was an achievement that it should have got so far, for at the beginning of the century the desert extended as far as where Tel Aviv itself now stands. Scattered about it were a few Arab villages, all impoverished and decadent. By the 1920s Jewish settlers had conquered the plain which leads from the desert to Rehovoth, specializing in the growing of oranges and grapes. Their luxuriant orange groves were already colouring the landscape a dark-green and in the spring pervading the region with the fragrance of the orange blossom. Everywhere, too, the regular rows of vines in numerous vineyards met the eye. But Rehovoth was the border town to the south; beyond that all was desert.

It was therefore a declaration of war on the desert when at Rehovoth, in 1933, Chaim Weizmann laid the foundation-stones of the establishment which today bears his name, the celebrated Weizmann Institute. From that day in 1933 a systematic work of research has been going on to conquer the Negev and tame the soil. It was a bold venture to set up a scientific institute in this poor pioneer land. In countries with old scientific traditions a new institute is merely a continuation of something already in progress. In Palestine, however, everything had to be built up from scratch. Had the attempt failed, there would have been repercussions in every section of Palestine's Jewish community. At the same time, it was plainly necessary to start something of the kind, if there was to be any hope at all of cultivating the Negev.

Briefly the object of the Weizmann Institute is to find new means of cultivating the land and of establishing industry. Both aims must be achieved in order to absorb the numerous immigrants who have already come and the still more that are expected. Agriculture is not enough; it does not provide sufficient employment, and the market for foodstuffs is highly fluctuating. But how to build up industries in a country so sparingly provided with natural resources? Two of the three requirements of heavy industry—coal, metals, and oil—are almost totally absent; the third is in its first stages of development.

Progress seems to envisage a combination of agriculture and industry, using new methods that will enable agricultural products to be converted into industrial raw materials. During the First World War Weizmann had discovered a process which enabled the war industry to extract acetone from maize and potatoes by fermentation. Now the Weizmann Institute is conducting research designed to convert sugar, starch, and cellulose into the same industrial materials which elsewhere are extracted from oil or coal. The castor bush is used for producing plastic; experiments are being made with synthetic rubber; new plants are being found that can be grown in arid regions like the Negev and used for the manufacture of paper, rope, or synthetic wood. Research is also being carried out on the exploitation of solar energy, the de-salting of sea-water, and much else. Rehovoth has long been an important centre for cancer research; research has gone into the peaceful uses of atomic energy and a reactor has been established.

But Israel's principal 'raw material' is its human material. In the 1930s, immediately after the establishment of the Weizmann Institute, a number of German scientists went there, when they found not only an asylum but a place which had need of their services. Someone has recently said:

'Because our country is poor in raw materials, in land and water, its future lies with its people. We must educate them and raise them to the highest possible level. It will not be a campaign of a hundred hours like Sinai; it will be a hard, daily battle for economic independence.'

On the day when the department of nuclear physics was inaugurated at Rehovoth, a visitor inquired about the distance from the nearest enemy air base.

'Six minutes' flying time,' was the reply.

'But,' the speaker added, 'it is nearly 2000 miles to the nearest institute that can compare with this one.'

The exchange emphasizes a remarkable fact which impresses itself upon every observant visitor to Israel. From the University at Givath Ram one looks across the adjacent frontier into the hostile country of Jordan. The whole of the Jewish side of Jerusalem is within firing range. So is Tel Aviv, and indeed every square yard of Israeli soil. Rehovoth and its costly institute can be bombed out of existence in a few minutes. Yet in spite of these grim possibilities the country is building a University, laboratories, libraries, institutes—all vulnerable things that cannot hit back, scientific centres in the firing line. It calls for both courage and faith to risk and to sacrifice so much in order to achieve a standard surpassed only in bigger countries remote from the Middle East. It is the same faith in the future which leads Israel to plant trees; only those who are sure of the future plan forests. But Israel has a still stronger faith in knowledge and is sowing it abundantly in the minds of her citizens. Here is a people with an obstinate belief in the survival of new generations which, with ideas and minds whetted since childhood and adolescence, have the ability not only to build up their own country, but also to bridge the gap to those who today are their implacable foes.

We have surveyed some of the peaks of Israeli cultural life. Several summits are visible from a distance, and the University of Jerusalem and the Weizmann Institute will stand out as typical examples. But it should be remembered that the ordinary people live their lives in the valley, and that the foundations of general culture are laid in the schools. Anyone who wants to study the main springs of Israeli life should sit on a school bench in a remote *kibbutz*, where the teacher sings with his class or sets them their lesson. The Jews have always been book-readers. For centuries studies were their principal pursuit, and learning is more highly regarded than riches. For this reason, Judaism has consistently emphasized child education, the main object being, not the one-sided imparting of knowledge, but the spiritual purpose of teaching. It is necessary to bear this in mind in order to understand the disputes on the problems of education which rage in Israel.

On one thing, however, all parties are united and that is that school attendance should be compulsory. The law which provides for this was passed by the Knesset immediately after the war in 1948. This was a revolution to the Arabs, who had only sent their boys to school when they had no use for them in the day-to-day work, and girls never. To the average Arab it was incomprehensible, and indeed repugnant, that girls should be educated. A woman's status in the old Arab community is so subordinate that it is thought injurious to her to possess knowledge. But in time the great majority of Arabs in Israel have come to accept the law on compulsory education.

Numerically, the Israeli education system has undergone an enormous development. Between 1948 and 1958 the number of pupils jumped from 100,000 to 500,000. This tremendous development was of course connected with the mass immigration; the great majority of Oriental immigrants have large families. It has led to many problems. In these few short years the country has had to provide accommodation, equipment, and teachers for a five-fold growth. In many places the conditions were primitive. The schools were huts of corrugated iron or sacking; the children sat on planks laid over boulders, or on the ground. It was necessary to improvise; but the authorities were able to muddle through, and now Israel, generally speaking, has organized her education system or at least its general framework.

We come now to the educational dispute. After interminable debate, the Knesset in 1949 enacted the remarkable education system which was in force during the early years and which astonished every foreign visitor. There was not one education system but four, each of them directed and controlled by a political party. The four streams were sharply divided and bitterly opposed. The widest gulf has been that between the Socialist schools of the Histadrut and the schools of the religious parties.

The rivalry between them had political consequences. When hundreds of thousands of new immigrants suddenly poured into the country the various groups, in reality the political parties, endeavoured to win over as many of their children as possible to them. In the reception camps there was a struggle for souls, a fight for the future. How would electors think and vote in ten, twenty, perhaps a hundred years? Other countries have, or have had, their cultural wars. In Israel, if one ever breaks out, it will be on such a scale that the nation will be split from top to bottom. The school dispute was felt to be the first sharp puff of a storm everyone wants to avoid, or at least delay in the hopes of mitigating it.

To the Jewish people religion is a factor of such real importance that religious neutrality is difficult, not to say impossible. Jewish religion is not a Sunday—or Sabbath—affair, as it often is in Christian countries: it permeates daily life from first to last. This means that an Orthodox teacher adopts religious views not only in scripture and history lessons, but also in subjects like mathematics and geology. And no teacher can avoid committing himself, one way or the other, with regard to the Bible. It is at once the religious and the classical Jewish book. The question is whether, when its ideas are being expounded in school, it is to be taken as the former or the latter. The subject is dynamite.

After some years of continual dispute, the Government succeeded in working out a *modus vivendi* between the Mapai and the Orthodox. The educational structure was simplified and now only two State-aided forms of education—general and religious—are recognized. Parents can choose freely between them. Both systems are supervised by the Ministry of Education, which is itself divided into two departments, responsible respectively for the two systems. Other schools receive no State support and tend, therefore, to languish. The agreement proved, however, to be only a temporary truce. The Orthodox wished to have the arrangement extended to higher education, and the debate got involved with other religious matters, and a Government crisis followed. The upshot was that the Orthodox withdrew their Ministers from the Government. The question remains unsettled.

In one respect, however, the schools are non-controversial and constitute a unifying factor. All teaching is in the Hebrew tongue, which is now the official language.

'These four are one: The Lord God, His people, the land of Israel, and the *Torah*.'

This is a quotation from the Talmud. But Eliezer ben Yehuda placed his own interpretation on it. As he saw it, the *Torah*, or in other words the Bible, was the title-deed to the land, given to His people by the Lord. But the right to the property becomes real only if the language of the deeds is spoken in the cities and by the rivers and mountains and shrines which since ancient times have borne Hebrew names. It follows that the new inhabitants of the old land must speak Hebrew.

This Eliezer ben Yehuda, as a young man, came with his newly wedded wife Deborah to Palestine in 1882, from a small ghetto-like town near Vilna. The father of the young man was called Yehuda Perlman, so that it is thus fairly easy to see why he afterwards took the name Ben Yehuda: it means 'Son of Yehuda'. The boy was educated in the traditional Jewish way according to the Law. But discovering that there was another world besides, he began to read its books, the first being none other than a Hebrew translation of *Robinson Crusoe*. He was found out, and was taught that it was a sin for a Jewish boy to venture outside the Law. The Bible and the Talmud were the only permitted books. He was severely punished and the boy ran away from home. That was the beginning; *Robinson Crusoe* in Hebrew had sown an intense love of the Hebrew language in this unusual boy's mind.

Ben Yehuda succeeded in finding people who would look after him, and eventually he arrived in Paris, where he began to study medicine with the object of becoming a doctor in Palestine. He was a sick man, subject to haemorrhages, yet with a will of iron he persisted. He *had to* live, for he had found his life's work: the revival of the Hebrew language and the teaching of his people to speak it. In early youth he had collected Hebrew words, writing them down on slips of paper to form material for a dictionary of Old and New Hebrew. When they sailed for Jaffa he confided in his bride his unshakable resolution, which was that in their future home in Jerusalem they should speak no other language but Hebrew, and that if they had children they, too, should speak Hebrew. In spite of poverty and persistent ill-health, Ben Yehuda realized his intention. His children were the first for thousands of years to speak in the nursery the language of the Bible, and whose first simple words were Hebrew ones. Meanwhile, Ben Yehuda undertook, alone and unaided, the immense scholarly labour of reviving long-forgotten words and forming new ones, so that the language might be revitalized. A whole academy of languages could not have done more than he did. In order to appreciate his achievement we must consider for a moment the diversity of problems which faced him and those who in time rallied round him.

The Old Testament world died 2500 years ago, and at the same time Hebrew ceased to be a vernacular language. Preserved in Holy Writ, it was a fossilized monument to a remote epoch in world civilization. In modern times its only significance has lain in the religious and humanistic ideas which it embodied. Living languages of the present day have evolved in pace with modern civilization, forming new expressions for new things and ideas as they arose. To become a vernacular language once more, Hebrew has had to leap 2500 years of history. It readily expresses abstract ideas, spiritual matters, matters of faith and doubt, of God and man. But when speaking of everyday matters, say of livestock and farm implements, one has to grope for the words and make artificial paraphrases. Reviving Hebrew is like building a house and beginning with the chimney at the top.

All this was argued by Ben Yehuda's critics, who also drew attention to Yiddish. This is a Jewish dialect, its name being derived from the German for 'Jewish'; it has developed along with the Jewish people, through all their varying fortunes, and is the daily language of millions. It can express all that Hebrew is incapable of expressing, and is a rare instrument for the rendering of Jewish ideas, the experiences of everyday life, and the ordinary emotions of love and hate, joy and grief. There is also a vigorous Yiddish literature, embracing novels, plays, folklore, and aphorisms.

'No,' was Ben Yehuda's reply, and soon that of most other Jews in Palestine, 'Yiddish was the language of our gaol. When a man comes out of prison he wants to forget its associations. The language of liberty is Hebrew.'

Nor is it strictly true that Hebrew was a dead language; for though Jews do not use Hebrew colloquially, they all speak it three times a day in their prayers. Religious instruction, too, is oral, as the pupils repeat their teachers' words in chorus as an aid to remembering them. When in the past Jews travelled abroad they would seek out their own people, and if they could not speak their language they possessed a common tongue in Hebrew. A vast number of books in Hebrew have survived the long centuries of exile. In Spain, and in Germany and France, Jews wrote letters, contracts, and receipts in Hebrew; the official correspondence between communities was also in Hebrew; the poets and philosophers were translated into it. Indeed, only books thus translated were looked upon as genuine Jewish works. Even when a Jew wrote in another language he would use the Hebrew letters.

In short, it had been an over-simplification to say that Hebrew was a dead language. It was alive, but stunted. One might say that Ben Yehuda and his fellows were reviving something which had suffered from malnutrition. Their problem was one of encouraging the flow of fresh sap and turning the streams of new life into old channels, in short, of bringing Hebrew up to date. So, since the death of Ben Yehuda a Hebrew Academy in Jerusalem has been engaged in rediscovering old words and creating new ones for the expression of new ideas.

There are many problems involved in thus rejuvenating an ancient language. David and Jeremiah knew nothing about aeroplanes or television, and there are many more shades of meaning in modern thought and language than were known to the ancients. Yet it is desired that New Hebrew (Ivrith, as it is called) should be employable in every field. People are giving Hebrew forms to their names; thus David Grün was turned into David Ben-Gurion, Shertok into Sharett. It has been said that Israel needs not only a *Who's Who?* but also a *Who Was Who?* Engineers from the former British oil refinery at Haifa found a new task in translating hundreds of technical terms into

Hebrew, *refining* the language, as they said. Some amusing cases are reported. Professor Tur-Sinai, a prominent philologist, president of the Hebrew Academy, and the man who is completing Ben Yehuda's dictionary, was asked by Ben-Gurion if he did not intend to turn the word 'academy' itself into Hebrew. The learned professor, however, retorted that this word was originally of Hebrew origin. Classical Greek took it from a man called Academos; but, Tur-Sinai says, the man must have been a Jew, since his name derives from a Hebrew root, *kedem*.

It is a fact that, in spite of all practical difficulties and unintentionally humorous results, Hebrew is now being spoken in Israel. The language of the love poems of the Song of Songs and the Law of Moses, of David and of Isaiah, can now be heard on the lips of bus conductors, farmers, and statesmen. It has become a new and vital tongue, used by frontier patrols, by road workers, and children at play, and diplomats. More than any other factor, it fuses the scattered tribes in the melting-pot of Israel into a nation.

Culture should not be confined to the few; but should reach out beyond the narrow circle of University people. In Israel it does. Schools, libraries, theatres, broadcasting, the Press, study groups, concerts, exhibitions: all that we understand by cultural life flourishes more vigorously than in most other countries. In Allenby Street in Tel Aviv I have counted more than a hundred places where books or other reading matter may be purchased. I have often been impressed to see the best of the world's literature, in four or five languages, on a farmer's bookshelves. And they are read.

Interest concentrates on youth, on children; the future belongs to them. The country teems with children, who grow up in sunshine and on orange juice and are robust and good-looking— as well as noisy. They sing so the houses reverberate; there are no muted strings here, nothing to be afraid of; they are at home in their own country.

'My boy will have a harder time here than he would if I had

gone to America,' a Ministerial official said to me. 'And in twenty years' time he won't have much to boast about to a Jewish-American boy of his own age. But he'll be proud of being an Israeli.'

And that is the point. The old air of the ghetto and the habitual Jewish outlook are gone; the uncertain, obsequious, and fearful have given way to pride and confidence.

'There are no Jews in this country, only Israelis,' they say. And history will one day tell of a people who stood alone with their backs to the sea and, fighting for their lives, succeeded in vanquishing their external enemies and conquering nature.

'*Jihjeh tov*,' is the usual remark when an Israeli concludes a discussion of current difficulties with a neighbour.

'It will be all right.'

Again the same outlook—the same faith.

WISDOM BUILT HERSELF A HOUSE

X

CONTRASTS

❦

ISRAEL is a land of contrasts. Small though it is, one of the
smallest countries in the world, it holds more differences
than any other country. From rugged mountains it drops
steeply to the deepest point in the world, the Dead Sea, 1290
feet below sea-level. Touring the country, one often sees the
sign: sea-level. It is an hour or two by car from the pure,
rarefied air of Galilee or Jerusalem to the oppressively humid
heat of Tel Aviv, or from the tropical climate of the Jordan
valley with its palms and banana plantations to the icy-cold
nights of Safad.

To describe this country one must use many and self-contra-
dictory words none of which expresses the quintessence of
Israel so that it comes alive in the imagination. Travelling
through it from Metulla to Eilat, one gains many varied
impressions: of tall eucalyptus trees with their deep, cool shade;
of slender, dark-green cypresses and silvery olive trees; of long
hedges of swelling, blue-green, and thorny cactuses sheltering
fragrant or golden-fruited groves: this whole luxuriance con-
trasting with waste, stony expanses caused by the erosion of
centuries. One day I stood in the mountains of Judah and across
the stagnant water of the Dead Sea saw the hills of Moab and
Edom turn reddish-brown and violet-blue in the dropping sun,
knowing that beyond them stretched the endless wilderness.
The next day I stood on the top of Carmel and saw the beautiful
Bay of Haifa with the blue water sparkling in the sun and,
far off along the coast to the north, Acre, the fortress of the

Crusaders, where the white spray washes the ancient walls set defiantly in the sea.

But it is also a country of ancient roads, which now pass hundreds of new village settlements with whitewashed and red-roofed houses or shacks of rusty corrugated iron; of new cities with modernistic architecture and busy traffic pulling up at traffic-lights; and of new roads which run through desert hills where no man ever trod before, and so on into great wildernesses.

Jerusalem and Tel Aviv are the oldest and the newest city in the world. I was with an engineer in a desolate region and I pointed to some crumbling ruins in the far distance.

'Those must be very old,' I exclaimed. He replied:

'No, they're new; only Byzantine.'

So old is this country which regards as new what is 'only' 1500 years old.

At the same time it is a country in the midst of the Atomic Age. In the shining white laboratories of Rehovoth scientists sit over test-tubes striving to solve the mystery of cancer, while the jet fighters roar overhead.

Perhaps this land of contrasts impresses its own character on the people to whom the Lord had promised it, the people who could never forget either the land or that promise? There seems, indeed, to be some sort of connection. At any rate I could describe the Jewish people, finding exact similes in the passing scenes. We find the same contrasts and potential conflicts in the Jewish mind as in the country's towering peaks and dark ravines. And perhaps they were the chosen people because God has always revealed Himself most clearly to minds in which Heaven and Hell are close and locked in mortal combat. It was the same David who as a red-cheeked boy came in from his father's flock to be anointed by the old prophet, and who was 'the man after God's heart', who became unforgettably great as king and prophet, but who afterwards coldly and calculatingly allowed Uriah to die. The Old Testament ranges from the bitter worldly wisdom of Ecclesiastes to the pastoral tones of the 23rd Psalm; and not only Yehuda Halevi and Spinoza were Jews, but also Karl Marx and Leon Trotsky.

As always, the contrasts are most obvious in matters of religion. And Jewish religion is full of great contrasts. We meet its extreme right wing at Mea Shearim in Jerusalem.

Mea Shearim is one of the oldest quarters of the Israeli part of the capital. The name is usually translated as 'The Hundred Gates', but that is incorrect. It means 'a hundred-fold' and it is used of the seed which gives a hundred-fold crop. Jews all over the world raised money with which to build Mea Shearim; boxes for contributions stood in thousands of synagogues and homes, and collections are still made in many places to maintain the pious scholars who live there. Here came the most devout Jews, not to live, but to die in the Holy City. They must not spend their days on practical work but must devote themselves to the study of the Law and the Talmud and so give a hundred-fold harvest for the gifts which provide their daily bread.

Life in Mea Shearim is passive and narrowly meditative; there is a sunset glow over it. In fact, it is a voluntary ghetto; its occupants segregate themselves completely from everyone else and are as hostile to people outside as their ancestors were to their Christian neighbours—and they to them. Here one does not have to imagine what daily life was like in the ghetto of the past; it displays itself before one's very eyes. Above the narrow, winding alleys clothes hung to dry drip down on to the heads of people from lines stretched from house to house; while shopkeepers and artisans sit on straw mats at open doors, arguing with their customers. The noise is drowned by the shrill voices of hawkers crying their wares. It is a teeming, chattering, boisterous life; we are indeed in the Orient.

Strangest of all, however, are the people. The men wear huge round hats with strips of fur (hence the name, *streimels*) and long black caftans reaching below the knees, with short trousers and long white or black stockings. The dress is intolerably hot and quite unsuitable for Palestine, but that was how people dressed in Poland in the seventeenth century and it would be thought irreverent to discard the garb of one's ancestors for the immodest present-day attire. The men grow their beards long, and both men and boys keep the hair at their temples in long twisted earlocks, called *payes*; for in the Law it says: 'Thou shalt not trim thy hair at the temples or cut thy beard.' The women walk behind the men; their heads are shaved after marriage, and they wear ugly wigs.

In Mea Shearim casuistic interpretations of the Law of Moses are maintained. The problems are studied and discussed and meditated upon deeply and at length. Handkerchiefs, for example, have been hotly debated. When nearly 2000 years ago, in thirty-nine articles, the Talmud prescribed what one must and must not do on the Sabbath, one of the things forbidden was to carry a burden. Handkerchiefs had not then been invented, so when they came into use it was an open question whether they were a part of the dress or a burden. In Mea Shearim they solve the problem by twisting the handkerchief round the belt. It then belongs to the dress and may be carried.

Of course we shake our heads at such sophistries. But greater things occur in Mea Shearim; and to see the life there at its best we should go on a Friday evening just after sunset, when the Sabbath has made her entry and the devout bid her welcome from the house-tops. Bearded, festively dressed men, patriarchal figures all, proceed ceremoniously through the streets to the synagogue, and through the windows we catch glimpses of a festively laid table with lighted candles, the two loaves laid out, a bottle of wine standing ready.

One must have local knowledge or a guide, for it is difficult to find one's way about. There are innumerable synagogues (over a hundred), but they are hidden in back-yards or cellars, the way leading by narrow lanes and alleys, through gateways and up steep flights of steps. But if one spends the hour before the service in looking into as many different synagogues as there is time for, one leaps in minutes from one continent to another. The Yemenites sit on the floor, three or four of them stooping over the same book together; a custom derived from a country with few and handwritten books. The route passes by way of the carpeted synagogues of Bokhara and the Caucasus, and suddenly we are in the middle of the nineteenth century, in synagogues from Polish and Russian village ghettos, with grey, sombre colours; or in one of the synagogues of the ecstatic Hasidists, where the congregation expresses its joy by singing and performing chain-dances. In the midst of it all people come and go, talking between prayers and whispering the latest news from ear to ear. The synagogue was always the place where one heard the local news.

But apart from the picturesqueness and strangeness of its customs, Mea Shearim is a problem. This is the centre of N'turei Karta, the most exclusive and fanatical religious group in the country, which has often given the Government and the police trouble. The fact is, N'turei Karta does not recognize the State of Israel. Only the Messiah can raise the Jewish nation, and the ungodly Zionists delay His coming by their fraudulent inventions. Accordingly, they consistently refuse to have any dealings with the State they live in. Hebrew is the sacred language, and it is profaned if used colloquially; in Mea Shearim they speak Yiddish. They do not use Israeli money, refuse to accept ration cards, and never send a letter by post; for that you need stamps, which imply a recognition of the State. On election day in 1959 the police had to remove Rabbi Amram Blau, one of these fanatics. The ageing, long-bearded rabbi had taken his stand in front of a polling booth. Not that he said anything about the impiety of voting; but he stared at everyone who approached the entrance, registering each one of them in his mind. They all knew that he would remember them and one day hurl curses on their heads if they ventured inside.

A state of war exists between Mea Shearim and the rest of Israel. Excited men range the town, throwing themselves in front of cars which dare to drive on Saturdays, breaking the Sabbath; or noting their numbers and sabotaging the cars on other days of the week, if they can, at parking places. One Saturday in September 1956 mass demonstrators blocked one of the main streets of Jerusalem, shouting in chorus: 'Sabbath, sabbath!' When the police tried to clear the street there was fighting and seven badly injured policemen and seventy demonstrators had to be taken to hospital, where one of the latter died. There was an even worse demonstration when a children's club was opened just outside Mea Shearim. N'turei Karta was deeply shocked that boys and girls should play there together and took action to remove the scandal. Fighting columns, armed with sticks and stones, moved in to the attack, and to the sound of the ram's horn, the club was stormed. People still talk of 'the little war of Jerusalem', as the fight between police and demonstrators that day is popularly called. It was evening before the city again settled down. It goes without saying that the fanatics were unruly when Jerusalem City Council opened a swimming pool for mixed bathing. They interpret the name N'turei Karta quite literally as 'Defenders of the City'. On the last occasion some American sympathizers marched in demonstration to the White House.

The N'turei Karta adherents number only a few hundred, and of course they will never acquire any real importance. But they are so vocal that they cannot be ignored. The long history of the Jewish people has always known such people, and it is conceivable that, with all their excesses, by the very vigour and clamour with which they have asserted extremist views and traditions, they have had a greater importance than their numbers would suggest.

It need hardly be said that there are many intermediate positions in the contrasted religious life of Israel.

I was running downstairs on my first morning in Tel Aviv, into the street, when I came to a sudden stop. I had heard a strange sound, which turned out to be the chanting of morning prayers in Hebrew in one of the apartments. I also recall the young man with whom I shared a room in a *kibbutz*, and who every morning, as though by routine, put on his *teffelin* (the small capsules containing Biblical texts that are affixed to the arm and forehead), and wrapping himself in his shawl turned his head towards Jerusalem and began to pray. It was only on the first few occasions that I was surprised by this. It is so different from the shy Christian way of praying to God behind closed doors. Soon, however, I realized how naturally it comes, and how general it is.

The Hebrew Bible, the part which Christians call the Old Testament, is known as the *Tenak*, from the Hebrew initials for the Law, the Prophets, and the Scriptures. The *Tenak* is the most popular book in Israel, being virtually in every home in the country, where it is also read.

At the peak listening time every evening, just before the news, Kol Israel, the Israeli Radio, broadcasts the music to the words of Isaiah: 'From Zion goes out the revelation, from Jerusalem the word of the Lord.' And then an actor, always the same person, so that listeners become familiar with the style and diction, reads a chapter from the Bible. One hears then what a beautiful language Hebrew is; and he varies the reading so well and dramatizes so rightly and naturally that one realizes one is listening to God's own words.

On September 15, 1958, the Jewish New Year 5719 began; and on the same day Sheikh Abdullah Mohammed Abu Kish'k of Petah Tikvah became at one stroke the richest man in the country. He was the formal owner of two-thirds of the land in Israel and had honestly bought and paid for it the sum of fifty pounds! The contract was signed at a ceremony in the Chief Rabbinate of Jerusalem. This curious ceremony was an attempt to obey the Biblical commandment of the sabbatical year: 'Six years shall ye sow the land and gather in its crops, but in the seventh shall ye leave it untilled.'

Just as God rested on the seventh day, so the earth that is His property must have a year of rest, a *shmittah*. Like many of the Bible's commandments this is a form of hygiene. The fields need to lie fallow, if they are not to become exhausted. In this case the commandment also has a social object, which is to relieve the burden of the poor, who are allowed to take what grows of itself in the fields.

Israel does not wish to break the commandment; but if it is interpreted literally, the country will go bankrupt. For this reason all land was sold to a non-Jew, since a gentile's land is not affected by the commandment, and so Jews may cultivate it in the sabbatical year. The Chief Rabbi had approached all landowners in advance and been authorized to make this strange transaction by the great majority of them. It should be added that the contract contains a provision that after the end of the sabbatical year the land reverts to its original owner. This 'sale' did not settle the matter for the Orthodox. They covered over their ploughs with an awning, so that the work should not take place in the open but 'in a dwelling'. The strictest among the Orthodox took the commandment quite literally and allowed their land to lie fallow, obtaining all their food by growing vegetables in a tank with the aid of chemicals.

One may smile at these desperate attempts to observe the commandment formally and yet admit reality. But they indicate that the Bible is a vital force in the country.

It takes a good deal of influence to get a ticket for the annual finals of the Bible Quiz. Although the newish and very modern Mann Auditorium in Tel Aviv, which forms the setting for the event, can seat several thousand spectators, the tickets are snatched away almost before they are on sale. One must take comfort in the fact that the contest, which lasts from eight to one, is transmitted in full over Kol Israel. It is no exaggeration to say that the whole nation listens to the display of Biblical knowledge made by the contestants. It is not only specialists who know their Bible. I was sitting in a friend's car when he suddenly stopped at a curb, where a ten-year-old boy was standing, a solitary male among a crowd of girls. Opening the window my friend asked the group:

'Where, in the Bible, does it say that "on that day seven women shall take hold of one man"?'

He had hardly finished the question when the boy replied: 'In Isaiah.'

I looked up my Bible and found it, true enough, in Isaiah iv. 1.

One cannot, however, speak of Judaism without mentioning the Sabbath; for it is not only Mea Shearim which celebrates it. Everywhere in Israel it is apparent on Friday evening at sunset that the Sabbath is approaching. The busy traffic stops abruptly; cars, buses, trains quieten down. 'For six days shalt thou labour, but the seventh is God's,' and the Sabbath is much more in evidence than in England, or even Scotland. But the festivals, the majority of religious significance, are woven into the annual rhythm: the gay, riotous *Purim*; the Passover with its celebration table; and the sombre *Yom Kippur*, the great Day of Atonement, a Jewish parallel to Good Friday.

One cannot compile statistics of a nation's religious life, and it is scarcely possible to obtain a survey of the attendance at services in the synagogues; there are so many, most of them very small and well concealed. I have heard that twenty per cent of the population wear earlocks, if that is any guide. No, the assessment depends on one's own approach, and on many more or less casual impressions.

There are people in Europe and America who assert that the people of Israel have broken away from religious life, and that religion there finds refuge in small isolated enclaves, which become smaller and smaller as the rising generations abandon the faith of their childhood. In a few decades, Jewish religion will have vanished from the land once called Holy.

It is true that there are some, even wide circles in Israel that are remote from the faith of their forefathers. How should the people of Israel remain unaffected by the wave of secularization that has swept across the world since the Renaissance? And where Jews discard their faith, they do so consistently, becoming positively religious in their anti-religiousness—again one of the contrasts. Yet it is my impression that the effects of secularization have been less pronounced in Israel than in most other places where I have had opportunities of first-hand inspection. The idea that Israel is developing into a bastion of atheism is without real foundation.

'We call the country Eretz Israel; that means "the Land of Israel". And if we scratch only a little way into the ground, we find Israel.'

It was Moshe Sharett who said this to me. He had wanted to emphasize wittily, how archaeological investigations in Palestine repeatedly demonstrate that it has been, since ancient times, the land of the Jews. The words apply not only to the country; they are also true of the mentality of its people. Anyone who delves beneath the surface finds irrefutable evidence that it has been ploughed, for millennia, with the plough of religion. It will take more than a generation or two to eradicate it.

But this deep furrow of religion throws up the earth on both sides, leaving chasms and contrasts inside and out. In the foregoing pages we have considered some of the common features of Israeli religious life. We will now return to the differences and divisions.

The religiously-minded Israelis, or the Orthodox, as one usually calls them when talking of politics, have large common aims. Inscribed on their banner are the words: *Medinat Israel— Medinat Ha-tora* (The State of Israel is the State of the Law). When the constitutional issue is discussed (Israel has no real written Constitution), the Orthodox parties are sharply opposed. Israel, they say, already has a basic law; the Law of Moses given to the Jewish people by God Himself. That is sufficient, and not a jot of it can be altered. In other words, Israel must be considered a theocracy; to be governed solely by the law of God. In order to realize this idea, the Orthodox went into politics from the start and formed their own parties.

Parties, but not party; for though the Orthodox have common aims, they are deeply split on the ways and means of achieving them and the various groups quarrel bitterly about them. At every General Election there have been attempts to find common ground, but each time they have failed.

The large and inclusive Mizrah Party, which is easily the most influential of the Orthodox groups, having a strong and, in its relations with the parent party, very independent Labour movement, is sharply opposed to Agudat Israel. In its ideas this party is not unlike N'turei Karta, but it has, in contrast, adopted a positive policy towards the State and is represented in the Knesset. It has its own schools and an important Labour organization.

We have seen how Ben-Gurion and his Mapai party have

been closely associated with the Orthodox in coalition Governments, and also how the coalition has been repeatedly shaken by intense differences between the two parties. Each time the quarrels have been patched up the Orthodox have extracted concessions; and during the years they have helped to govern Israel they have won a fair number of points. Each time bitter strife preceded the concession.

I have already mentioned the disputes that are connected with the Education Act. National service for women has given rise to other difficulties. When it was proposed, religious leaders contended that it was in conflict with the Jewish faith and Jewish religious practice for women to serve as soldiers. The outcome was a compromise. It was agreed that a woman unable to serve for religious reasons should be exempted. Then three further issues arose and remain unsettled: the attitude to the Sabbath, the marriage law, and the question of what constitutes a Jew. The debate on these three matters throws an interesting light on Jewish religion.

Observance of the Sabbath is, of course, one of the ten commandments, and thus a demand which the Orthodox have no intention of relaxing. Yet wide circles in Israel want reforms of the Sabbath legislation. They think it wrong that public transport should be suspended on that day, so that ordinary people cannot get to the beach or to sports grounds, though people with cars can go wherever they like. They ridicule casuistic decisions by the rabbis to allow essential work to be done, such as the one which permitted a clerk to telegraph on the Sabbath provided that he used only his left hand and the Latin alphabet instead of the Hebrew. And what is one to say of work on public services, water and electricity supplies, and in hospitals?

Some people talk of reviving the supreme religious authority of the past, the Sanhedrin, and of convening a competent body which would decide on these and numerous similar problems. The dispute about the Sabbath is indeed a deeply serious one to the Orthodox; it is not an argument about details, but about the very character of the Jewish people.

The same applies to the legislation on marriage and divorce. Under the British Mandate marriages and divorces by Jews in Palestine were the responsibility of a Jewish religious court, and after the establishment of Israel the Knesset, under pressure from the Orthodox, retained the arrangement. It follows that there are no civil marriages in Israel, and that mixed marriages between, say, Jews and Christians are out of the question. Rabbinic law gives its permission only on condition that the non-Jewish partner adopts Judaism.

This is obviously an inflammable situation. There was a young artist who went on hunger strike when he was not allowed to marry his Christian fiancée. Even worse was the case of the boy who died of polio. He was the child of a mixed marriage, his mother being a non-Jew, and by Jewish tradition the child follows the mother. Thus the boy was non-Jewish, and he was refused burial inside the walls, the parents being obliged to bury him outside the burial ground.

The Orthodox will not yield an inch. To them the Jewish people and Jewish tradition are one, and family life has always been protected by the faith. If the marriage legislation is tampered with a deep split will occur in the Israeli nation. The religious will never recognize civil marriages, and children of such marriages are illegitimate, refused marriage to young people from religious families.

In 1958 there was a new crisis. The occasion seemed innocent enough. The Ministry of the Interior intended to issue new identity cards, and all were required to state their nationality. The Ministry said that it would be satisfied if a person declared, 'in good faith', that he was a Jew and did not belong to any other religion. The Orthodox members of the Government were furious. They maintained that it was certainly not a private matter whether one was a Jew or not. A question so fundamental can only be decided by a religious body, in this case the Chief Rabbinate in Jerusalem. The matter is not just an academic one, but affects hundreds, perhaps thousands, of people. The fact is that there are more mixed marriages in Israel than one at first sight discovers, especially among immigrants from

Poland, not a few of whom brought with them their Christian wives. Children of such marriages are not Jewish unless properly admitted into Judaism. The dispute coincided with the debate on the secondary schools, and in June 1958 it led to a Government crisis. The Orthodox Ministers resigned.

Yes, Israel is indeed the land of contrasts.

There is a further religious cleavage in Israel.

Since the State was established a remarkable number of Christian missionaries have come into the country; a veritable offensive, as the Orthodox see it. It has something to do with the great interest which the new State has aroused all over the world, though in wide circles of the Christian Church there has always been a deep desire to lead the Jews to the Christ they once rejected. Perhaps there is also the purely practical factor that China has recently been closed to Christian missions, so that new spheres of activity have had to be found. However that may be, many Christian missionaries are busily engaged in Israel; the Ministry for Religions has put them at not less than a 1000, of whom 200 are Protestants.

The first result has been a violent reaction by the Orthodox Jews. They have even begun to organize a counter-offensive and are endeavouring to enlist the support of the authorities. They declare that certain foreign missions, notably some rather business-minded American missionaries, employ rather smart methods, trying, they say, to 'purchase' souls in return for food parcels and clothes, or else tempting them with promises of visas to countries where the conditions are less austere than they are in Israel. The stipulated terms are baptism. As far as I am able to judge the charges—incredible to say—are, in a few isolated cases, true.

Clearly, however, no-one need fear such actions which do not affect the spirit, while people who can be bought are no loss. It looks worse from the Christian angle, but, there again, there is no need to waste many words on those concerned; only to say that they are not a good advertisement for Christianity.

What is important, is that Israel feels she needs a breathing-space. This small nation has been through such violent crises that it can hardly cope with any more. The assimilation of large numbers of immigrants from a diversity of countries requires that all should concentrate on unification. Because of this, the Israelis think it unfair that Christian missions should create further difficulties at this time, and they urge them to wait for a decade or two.

There is religious liberty in Israel and Christian missionaries are free to operate there, within certain limits at any rate, and they are also protected by the authorities. But feelings towards them are not very friendly, and they should beware of provocative behaviour. An American missionary rashly attended a meeting of the 'Anti-Defection Society', which is an extremely active anti-mission society. In the tumult which followed his discovery, he was thrown out. I have actually met secret Christians, people who know that if they are discovered they will be dismissed from their posts.

We Christians have learned to regard Judaism as a religion of the past. For their part, the Jews have such evil memories of Christian persecutions that their reaction to a cross is one of suspicion. But complacency means petrifaction, from which nothing can grow. Only the man who knows that he has 'never arrived but always travelling' has the receptive mind in which new seed can grow and flowers blossom.

The secret that lies hidden in the soul of the Jewish people is endless. Why have these people gone on existing? In the face of persecution and catastrophe and millennia of exile they have defiantly lifted up their heads and continued to live. No other people has displayed a similar will to live. Many rational explanations may be suggested, but always the mystery remains. I can think of only one ultimate explanation: the unfathomable, inexplicable, and unknowable mystery of what we call God's election.

He allowed these people to live, and he allowed them to live as Jews. It follows that—somehow or other, unrevealed to the half-blind creatures that we are—He has a further use for them, as if He is holding them in reserve for a purpose known only to Himself.

The two great religions, of Judaism and Christianity, went their different ways. Mother and daughter parted, and have remained on either side of an abyss that is so deep it has seemed unbridgable. We are too small for that; it will be done only when God wills it, and in the manner in which He wills it. But the day on which these two find each other the mother will have gifts for her daughter, and the daughter will whisper a secret that will gladden her mother's heart.

On that day all contrasts will meet.

XI

THE ROSE OF JERICHO

ॐ

THE *hamsin* was blowing for the third day, as hard and pitilessly as ever. The sweat streamed down foreheads and cheeks, and I felt it starting out on my whole body. But the heat was so intense that it at once dried off and one's clothes continued to feel dry. A desolate landscape lay outstretched before me, where the mountains of Hebron slowly fall into the level plain of the Negev. A month or two before, the country had burst into broad, coloured expanses. Late rains and spring sunshine had called forth the flowers—vivid red anemones, the Biblical lilies of the field, cyclamen, and white narcissi, or rose of Sharon; in marvellous radiance they shone in the strong sunlight. The splendour was short-lived; the summer sun and drought killed off the tender plants, and today I saw the last of them softly die away in the *hamsin*, a few withered leaves curling up, to crumble and disappear.

A dry, rustling sound caught my ear. Looking round to see where it came from, I saw, dancing over the stony ground, a small brown ball, bouncing light and round over stones and hopping across fissures. At first I thought it was a bird that had been alarmed by a hawk and was seeking cover and safety.

Suddenly I discovered that it was not alone; there were several, many dancing balls. Catching one of them I stood with it in my hand. I realized then that I had been mistaken; it was not a bird, but a withered seed-pod that the wind had been chasing. I put it into my bag, and that evening, at the hotel in

Beersheba, I heard its history. It is called the rose of Jericho and grows in the desert. When the rain moistens the dry earth the plant blossoms into small white flowers, delicate and tender. But as soon as the flowers die in the drought the dried parts roll up and close tightly round the fruit, so as to form a ball. The wind tears it loose from the root and blows it about, and it is heard to rattle each time it strikes a stone or is rolled over the ground. Hundreds of them may roll away together. But they are not dead; their withered brown capsule shelters the new life of next spring.

Before going to bed I placed the rose of Jericho in water. The next morning the flower had unfolded and now looked as it had looked when it had been young and fresh in the spring sunshine. The wind carries its protected seed to distant places; there, as soon as it finds moisture, it revives and grows into a new flower. It dies hard, for it has the will to live and to wait till the smallest means of life appears. For this reason there are those who call the rose of Jericho the resurrection flower; and there is no wonder that legends and traditions have become associated with it. The Virgin Mary found it during the flight into Egypt; seeing in it an omen of life and good fortune, she promised the flower everlasting life.

I saw the rose of Jericho as a symbol of the destiny of the Jewish people. In its tender spring it took root in the same Holy Land where the rose, too, belongs. Like it, Israel blossomed into the world's finest flowers during the long centuries when the blessing of God fell down on it like the rain. The world would have been empty had it not possessed the Bible and the revelation which the chosen people received and passed on to the rest of us.

But drought and storm set in. The gale whistled over Jerusalem, tearing the people from their roots, scattering them in thousands of years of exile, and tumbling them about the world. Israel never found a permanent rest; fathers seldom dared to hope that their sons would go on from where they themselves had left off. All was temporary and intermittent in Jewish history. But against all common sense the rose managed to survive, and if it found only the slightest possibility of moisture and life, it sprang into new flower. Jewish history is a continually repeated resurrection.

Other peoples have had to migrate and find new homes. But they lost their identity in a new environment, becoming assimilated into other nations. The Jews alone remained Jews; that is their unique history. Whenever the storm set them wandering, they shut themselves in, folded themselves up round their inner core, their faith and their tradition. Wherever they went they took this with them, waiting patiently until a means of fresh life presented itself. Then at once they unfolded themselves. Babylon, Spain, the Rhineland, Poland, America are stages on the long wandering. And each of these names heads an epoch of Jewish life, with a pronounced and individual culture.

'All things are in the hand of God, except the fear of God.'

So runs one of the doctrines of the Talmud. The fear of God is man's own responsibility and choice. There was always a hard core of Israel which never let go of the God who once chose it as His own people. They saw Him as the source of light and creator of darkness; and through many evil and few good days they clung to Him and handed as a precious inheritance from generation to generation: their faith and hope that at the right time He would turn their fate.

And after millennia of waiting the God who guides the destinies of men and nations caused the wind to blow in the direction of Jerusalem. The two generations before our own saw the rose of Jericho take a new course. First the few who were alert enough to feel the wind of change, and then the many: tens of thousands, hundreds of thousands, now over a million. It was the lot of our generation to see Israel strike root in the soil of its forefathers. It happened only twelve years or so ago. From Dan to Beersheba, from Beersheba to Eilat, the rose found its old place of growth.

Today the rose is unfolding on classical soil. And once again the world can expect remarkable gifts from the people who would never die, because their God wanted to keep them alive.

I recall a devout man in Jerusalem who took out the Book of Jeremiah and pointed to one of the promises in it:

'For I know the thoughts that I think toward you, saith the Lord, thoughts of peace and not of evil, to give you an expected end.'

INDEX

217

GEORGE ALLEN & UNWIN LTD
London: 40 Museum Street, W.C.1

Auckland: 24 Wyndham Street
Bombay: 15 Graham Road, Ballard Estate, Bombay 1
Buenos Aires: Escritorio 454–459, Florida 165
Calcutta: 17 Chittaranjan Avenue, Calcutta 13
Cape Town: 109 Long Street
Hong Kong: F1/12 Mirador Mansions, Kowloon
Ibadan: P.O. Box 62
Karachi: Karachi Chambers, McLeod Road
Madras: Mohan Mansions, 38c Mount Road, Madras 6
Mexico: Villalongin 32–10, Piso, Mexico 5, D.F.
Nairobi: P.O. Box 12446
New Delhi: 13–14 Asaf Ali Road, New Delhi 1
São Paulo: Avenida 9 De Julho 1138–Ap. 51
Singapore: 36c Prinsep Street, Singapore 7
Sydney, N.S.W.: Bradbury House, 55 York Street
Toronto: 91 Wellington Street West

RICHARD THE THIRD
PAUL MURRAY KENDALL

This can be called the first real biography of a notorious but actually unknown King, one of the most controversial figures in English history. Previous works, whether frankly popular or of scholarly stamp, have been largely devoted to arguing a 'case' either for or against King Richard. They have too often relied, if ardently defending him, on wishful speculation or have followed the Tudor tradition of history, now no longer tenable, of showing him to be the ruthless villain of Shakespeare's melodrama.

This biography offers an impartial study of Richard's enigmatic character and turbulent career. Based almost wholly upon the Pre-Tudor historical sources of Richard's own day, it includes much entirely fresh material as well as information unobtainable when the Gairdner biography was published. It removes Richard from the shadow of misrepresentation and rumour. It artfully shapes Richard's life into a drama of tragic passion and violence, complex in thematic development and fascinating in its psychology. It evokes the neglected but colourful times in which Richard lived and the array of great figures whose lives touched his—Warwick the Kingmaker, Margaret of Anjou, Louis the Eleventh, Edward the Fourth, Caxton, Jane Shore, Henry Tudor, and many others. A special section has been devoted to what is perhaps the most famous, and bitterly disputed, murder mystery in English annals —that of the 'little Princes in the Tower'.

This is one of the most readable works of history that has ever come into its publisher's hands.

'. . . this is the work of a true historian . . . a first-class piece of historical writing; and even if it is as interesting as a novel that does not mean that it is in any sense a work of fiction.' *The Sphere.*

'. . . really first-rate piece of biographical writing.' *Country Life.*

'This bustling, vivid, exuberant biography. . . . Mr Kendall has drawn a plausible, human and convincing picture of Richard and he has also told an exciting story with infectious enthusiasm and dramatic skill.' *The Daily Telegraph.*

'His sources are unimpeachable, his handling of them impeccable. The result is an invaluable picture of Richard both as a man and a king. . . . Sheer scholarship apart, the strongest point of this book is that Richard is not placed in the dock.' *Glasgow Herald.*

Fourth Impression. Illustrated. Sm. Royal. 8vo. 35s. net

THE YORKIST AGE
PAUL MURRAY KENDALL

The Yorkist Age unfolds the panorama of daily life during the Wars of the Roses. This first full-length study of English society in the fifteenth century draws upon contemporary narratives of travellers, the Paston Letters and other less widely known collections of correspondence, observations of French and Italian diplomats, town records, ecclesiastical reports, the literature of the age, chronicles, household and estate accounts, wills, chancery proceedings, and other revealing sources, in order to recreate the substance and the flavour of the life of the time.

Ideas, attitudes, fears, aspirations, the 'olde daunce' of love and death, as well as the dress of the age, housekeeping in town and country, recreation and the state of business and the way of courtship are caught in action, as they display themselves in the histories, proud and humble of hundreds of people.

Contrary to Shakespeare and popular belief, the Wars of the Roses had comparatively little effect upon the lives of the people as a whole and represented rather a recovery from than a descent into anarchy. The story of modern England opens not with the Tudors but in this Yorkist realm, a fascinating period of beginnings-and-endings, prosperously balanced between the upheavals of the late fourteenth century and the hard times and hard feelings of the early sixteenth.

Illustrated. Demy 8vo. 35s. net

ASIA AND WESTERN DOMINANCE
K. M. PANIKKAR

Leading reviews from the world's press greeted the appearance of this classic study of history. For the first time we had a view from a brilliant Asian historian of the political events which led to the subjection of Asia. 'Its publication is a political as well as a literary event. The book is quite free from the xenophobic desire to restore the dead past in Asia. Panikkar counts up the profit which Asia gained from subjection, as well as the humiliation which it suffered.'—*The Manchester Guardian.*

Fifth Impression. Demy 8vo. Cloth 25s. net. Paper 18s. net

WARWICK THE KINGMAKER
PAUL MURRAY KENDALL

Richard Neville, Earl of Warwick—called the Kingmaker—has been relegated to a famous oblivion. Is there any other man in English history so well known and so little known about? The chronicles of his age recorded his deeds and registered his impact, but passing time has been cruel to whatever revelations of himself were left in his restless wake. Tudor writers were so intent on depicting the victory of Henry Tudor as part of the pattern of God's justice, that Warwick was regarded only as a bellicose baron in the hurly-burly of civil strife from which England had been rescued. Thus, from the Elizabethan Age until recent times, no one thought it worth while to attempt his biography. Professor Oman's *Life* (1891), until now the only reputable work, is really a history of Warwick's times and deeds, and tells us little about the man himself.

Paul Kendall, whose biography of Richard III received such high praise in 1955, has attempted to make good this deficiency. The result is a work of historical biography every bit as colourful and dynamic as its predecessor. This picture of a turbulent age and of the warrior who bestrode it has a grip on the reader that never relaxes from first to last. For the first time in literature Warwick, the last of the barons, becomes a figure of flesh and blood, and a memorable human being.

'It can be said at once that Mr Kendall's new book is lively, interesting and learned. He has taken a great deal of trouble to establish his facts, he writes with zest, and he knows how to shape a fascinating narrative, and he can communicate his own genuine feeling for the atmosphere of this remote age.' *Birmingham Post*.

'The story of the Wars of the Roses is, after all, an exciting story, full of the most dramatic vicissitudes of fortune, and it loses nothing by being retold with this splendidly emblazoned lay figure at the centre of it.' *The Times*.

Illustrated. Sm. Royal. 8vo., 30s. net

DAILY LIFE IN FRANCE UNDER NAPOLEON
JEAN ROBIQUET

Demy 8vo. 35s. net

THE ASIAN CENTURY

PROFESSOR JAN ROMEIN
University of Amsterdam

Translated from the German by R. T. CLARK

The last hundred years have seen the transformation of Asia. In the north Russia has absorbed the old Moslem states and has civilized Siberia; in the south-east and south-west former 'colonial' territories—the Middle East under Turkey, India and Ceylon under Britain, Indo-China under France, and Indonesia under the Dutch—are now free and independent. China is now Communist; old countries like Persia and Siam have entered the mainstream of international life; Turkey is a secular republic; Japan's bid for empire has failed; and Britain has abandoned Egypt to an ambitious dictator.

Asia has also suffered a social and industrial revolution which is still in progress. This development has been followed with passionate interest by a Dutch historian, Professor Romein, who knows south-east Asia at first hand. His book is mainly concerned with this area, but he includes also Turkey, China and Japan. He sees the revolution under a variety of aspects, initially as a struggle against 'colonialism' and a reaction against the West, seen as much in imitation as in resistance to its domination. Each country's answer to the problems confronting it is carefully analysed, whether arising from the desire for independence or from the onset of the great technological changes of our times whereby nations moved from a peasant to an industrial economy, changes which coincided in time with the revelation of Western weakness in two World Wars.

Professor Romein sees the Asian century as over in the sense that Asia is now free of foreign domination, a victory which has created more problems for the new states than it has solved. Asia is still 'on the march' to a future which it is difficult to foresee. If Professor Romein is frankly 'anti-colonial', he is equally frank about those who in Asia led the fight against it and have now the full responsibility for what he sees as a race against time. No one who is aware of the importance of Asia in the contemporary world can neglect his account of an astounding transformation accomplished in relatively so short a time.

Demy 8vo. 50s. net